# JOIN-AS-YOU-GO
# AFGHANS™

The Needlecraft® Shop

**EDITOR** Bobbie Matela

**ART DIRECTOR** Brad Snow

**PUBLISHING SERVICES MANAGER** Brenda Gallmeyer

**ASSOCIATE EDITORS** Kathy Wesley, Mary Ann Frits

**ASSISTANT ART DIRECTOR** Nick Pierce

**COPY SUPERVISOR** Michelle Beck

**COPY EDITORS** Mary O'Donnell, Beverly Richardson

**TECHNICAL ARTISTS** Liz Morgan, Nicole Gage

**GRAPHIC ARTS SUPERVISOR** Ronda Bechinski

**BOOK DESIGN** Brad Snow

**GRAPHIC ARTISTS** Glenda Chamberlain, Edith Teegarden

**PRODUCTION ASSISTANTS** June Sprunger, Marj Morgan, Cathy Reef

**PHOTOGRAPHY** Tammy Christian, Carl Clark, Christena Green, Matthew Owen

**PHOTO STYLISTS** Tammy Nussbaum, Tammy Smith

**CHIEF EXECUTIVE OFFICER** John Robinson

**PUBLISHING DIRECTOR** David McKee

**EDITORIAL DIRECTOR** Vivian Rothe

**MARKETING DIRECTOR** Dan Fink

**FIRST PRINTING** 2005

**LIBRARY OF CONGRESS CONTROL NUMBER** 2005920832

**HARDCOVER ISBN** 1-57367-199-1

**SOFTCOVER ISBN** 1-57367-216-5

Printed in China

Every effort has been made to ensure the accuracy and completeness of the instructions in this book. However, we cannot be responsible for human error or for the results when using materials other than those specified in the instructions, or for variations in individual work.

Retail outlet owners and resellers: For additional copies of this book call (800) 772-6643.

1 2 3 4 5 6 7 8 9

# CONTENTS

# INTRODUCTION

We are so excited about this collection of afghans we can hardly wait to share them!

We asked our favorite designers to create afghans that can be joined as they are crocheted. This means that once you have finished crocheting all the motifs or panels, you are really finished.

Since the motifs are added one after the other you won't have a pile of motifs that need tedious sewing together. And afghans made in panels are added as you are crocheting as well.

So the good news is, once you are finished crocheting you are really ready to enjoy your afghan.

We have divided our 47 afghans into 8 chapters to make it easier to find just the right design to fit the occasion.

Welcoming Garden and Fantasy Flowers offer designs with florals and gentle garden themes.

Cool Squares are new, innovative looks that are done in squares and rectangles.

Furry Frenzy utilizes a new textured yarn in each design.

Delightful Dimensions includes out-of-the-ordinary afghans that have 3-D interest.

Child's Play is the chapter for babies' and kids' comfort throws or shower gifts.

Seasonal Pleasures have been designed to display for a holiday or season.

And Mood Monochrome contains restful afghans that are created using all one color or different shades of one color.

Glad you are joining us for some great crochet fun!
Happy Stitching,

*Bobbie Matela*

*Kathy Wesley*

# WELCOMING GARDEN

These gentle designs will lend a graciousness to your surroundings or can be given as thoughtful, loving gifts.

# SUNNY DAY FLOWERS

Design by Diane Poellot

## FINISHED SIZE
Approximately 54 x 70 inches

## MATERIALS
- Red Heart Super Saver medium (worsted) weight yarn (8 oz/452 yds/226g per skein): 3 skeins #320 cornmeal (E), 2 skeins #632 medium sage (F), 1 skein each #316 soft white (G), #358 lavender (C), #774 light raspberry (A), #347 light periwinkle (D)
- Red Heart Classic medium (worsted) weight yarn (3½ oz/198 yds/99g per skein): 2 skeins #252 medium coral (B)
- Size J/10/6mm crochet hook or size needed to obtain gauge

## GAUGE
Rnds 1–3 of motif = 4 inches square
To save time, take time to check gauge.

## SPECIAL STITCHES
For **3-double crochet cluster (3-dc cl):** Keeping last lp of each dc on hook, work 3 dc in same sp or st, yo and draw through all 4 lps on hook.

For **4-double crochet cluster (4-dc cl):** Keeping last lp of each dc on hook, work 4 dc in same sp or st, yo and draw through all 5 lps on hook.

For **joining ch-3 sp:** Ch 1, sl st in corresponding ch-3 sp on motif indicated, ch 1.

## PATTERN NOTE
Join with slip stitch unless otherwise stated.

## FIRST ROW
### FIRST MOTIF
**Rnd 1:** With G, ch 4, join with sl st to form ring, ch 4 *(counts as dc and ch-1)*, (dc, ch 1) 7 times in ring, join in 3rd ch of beg ch-4. *(8 dc, 8 ch sps)* Fasten off.

**Rnd 2:** Join flower color (A, B, C or D according to diagram) with sc in any ch-1 sp, ch 1, **3-dc cl** *(see Special Stitches)* in same sp, *ch 3, **4-dc cl** (see Special Stitches) in next ch sp; rep from * 6 times more, ch 3, join in top of 3-dc cl. Fasten off. *(8 ch-3 sps)*

**Rnd 3:** Attach F with sc in any ch-3 sp, ch 2, (2 dc, ch 3, 3 dc) in same sp, [ch 5, sk next ch sp, (3 dc, ch 3, 3 dc) in next ch sp] 3 times, ch 5, join in 2nd ch of beg ch-2. Fasten off.

**Rnd 4:** Attach E with sc in any ch-3 sp, ch 3, sc in same sp, *ch 3, working in front of Rnd 3, 5 dc in ch-3 sp of Rnd 2, ch 3, (sc, ch 3, sc) in next ch-3 sp; rep from * twice more, ch 3, working in front of Rnd 3, 5 dc in ch-3 sp of Rnd 2, ch 3, join in first sc. Fasten off.

## SECOND ROW
### FIRST MOTIF
Work same as First Motif on First Row referring to Assembly Diagram for flower color.

### SECOND MOTIF
Referring to Assembly Diagram for flower color, work Rnds 1–3 of First Motif on First Row.

**Rnd 4 (motif joining):** Attach E with sc in any corner ch-3 sp, **joining ch-3 sp** *(see Special Stitches)* in corresponding corner of previous row, sc in same ch-3 sp on working motif, joining ch-3 sp in next ch-3 sp of previous motif, working in front of Rnd 3 on working motif, 5 dc in next ch-3 sp of Rnd 2, joining ch-3 sp in next ch-3 of previous motif, sc in corner ch-3 of working motif, joining ch-3 sp in ch-3 sp of previous motif and corresponding corner motif of motif on previous row, sc in same corner ch-3 sp on working motif, joining ch-3 sp in next ch-3 sp of previous motif, working in front of Rnd 3 on working motif, 5 dc in next ch-3 sp of Rnd 2, joining ch-3 sp in next ch-3 of previous motif, sc in corner ch-3 of working motif, joining ch-3 sp in ch-3 sp of previous motif, sc in same sp on working motif, ch 3, working in front of Rnd 3, 5 dc in next ch-3 sp on Rnd 2, ch 3, (sc, ch 3, sc) in next ch-3 sp, ch 3, working in front of rnd 3, 5 dc in next ch-3 sp on Rnd 3, ch 3; join in first sc. Fasten off.

## REMAINING ROWS

Referring to Assembly Diagram for flower color and motif placement, work rem motifs as for Second Motif in Second Row joining to adjacent motifs in similar manner.

## BORDER

Holding afghan with one short end at top, join E with an sc in first dc of 5-dc group as shown on Assembly Diagram, sc in next dc, (sc, ch 3, sc) in next dc, sc in next 2 dc, sc in next ch, *[ch 1, sk next 2 chs, sc in next sc, (2 sc, ch 3, 2 sc) in corner ch-3 sp, sc in next sc, ch 1, sk next 2 chs, sc in next ch, sc in next 2 dc, (sc, ch 3, sc) in next dc, sc in next 2 dc,

sc in next ch, ch 1, sk next 2 chs, sc in next sc, dc in motif joining, sc in next sc, ch 1, sk next 2 chs, sc in next ch, sc in next 2 dc, (sc, ch 3, sc) in next dc, sc in next 2 dc, sc in next ch] 7 times, ch 1, sk next 2 chs, sc in next sc, (2 sc, ch 3, 2 sc) in corner ch-3 sp, sc in next sc, ch 1, sk next 2 chs, sc in next ch, sc in next 2 dc, (sc, ch 3, sc) in next dc, sc in next 2 dc, sc in next ch, rep between [ ] 10 times, ch 1, sk next 2 chs, sc in next sc, (2 sc, ch 3, 2 sc) in corner ch-3 sp, sc in next sc, ch 1, sk next 2 chs, sc in next ch**, sc in next 2 dc, (sc, ch 3, sc) in next dc, sc in next 2 dc, sc in next ch, rep from * ending at **; join in first sc.

Fasten off and weave in all ends. 🐦

**Sunny Day Flowers**
Assembly Diagram

# ROSES ARE BLUE

Design by Carol Alexander

## FINISHED SIZE
Approximately 42 x 56 inches

## MATERIALS
- Red Heart Super Saver medium (worsted) weight yarn (8 oz/452 yds/225g per skein): 4 skeins #0334 buff (D), 3 skeins #0316 soft white (C), 1 skein each #0382 country blue (A) and #0380 Windsor blue (B)
- Size H/8/5mm crochet hook or size needed to obtain gauge

## GAUGE
Rnds 1–11 of motif = 7 inches square
To save time, take time to check gauge.

## SPECIAL STITCHES
For **treble cluster (tr cl):** Keeping last lp of each tr on hook, 4 tr in st indicated, yo, draw through all 5 lps on hook.
For **picot:** Ch 3, sl st in top of last dc made.

## PATTERN NOTE
Join with slip stitch unless otherwise stated.

## FIRST MOTIF
**Rnd 1:** With A, ch 6, join to form ring, working over beg yarn tail, ch 1, 24 sc in ring, join in **front lp** of first sc.

**Rnd 2 (flower center):** Working in **front lps** only of Rnd 1, [ch 3, sk next sc, sl st in next sc] 12 times, ending with last sl st at base of beg ch-3. Fasten off. *(12 ch-3 lps)*

**Rnd 3:** Attach B in the **back lp** of any sc of Rnd 1, ch 4 *(counts as a dc and ch-1 sp)*, [dc in same sp, ch 1] 4 times, dc in same sp, turn *(WS of work now facing)*, sl st in 3rd ch of beg ch-4 (inserting hook through back of st), turn *(RS of work now facing)*—petal made, *ch 3, sk next 2 sc on Rnd 1, [dc in **back lp** of next sc, ch 1] 5 times, dc in same sc, turn, sl st in 3rd ch of ch-3, turn; rep from * 7 times, ending sl st in back first petal. Fasten off. *(8 petals)*

Pull beg yarn tail at center of flower tightly to close center opening to ¼ inch. Weave in end and secure on back of flower. Arrange petals and center ch lps evenly around.

**Rnd 4:** Working behind petals, attach C to lp joining edges at bottom center of any petal, ch 1, sc in same sp, ch 4, [sc in lp at bottom center of next petal, ch 4] 7 times, join in first sc. *(8 ch-4 sps)*

**Rnd 5 (leaves):** *(Sl st, ch 4, **tr cl** {see Special Stitches}, ch 2, sl st between 2nd and 3rd tr of tr cl, ch 4, sl st) in next ch-4 sp; rep from * 7 times more. Fasten off. *(8 leaves)*

**Rnd 6:** Working behind leaves, attach D in the **back lp** of sc on Rnd 4 between any 2 leaves, ch 1, sc in same place, ch 7, sk next sc of Rnd 4, [sc in **back lp** of next sc, ch 7, sk next sc] 3 times, join in first sc. *(4 ch-7 sps)*

**Rnd 7:** Sl st in first ch-7 sp, ch 4 *(counts as tr)*, 9 tr in same sp, ch 4, [10 tr in next ch-7 sp, ch 4] 3 times, join in 4th ch of beg ch-4.

**Rnd 8:** Ch 1, sc in same st as joining, hdc in next tr, dc in next 2 tr, 2 dc in next tr, **picot** *(see Special Stitches)*, 2 dc in next tr, dc in each of next 2 tr, hdc in next tr, sc in next tr, 5 sc in next ch-4 sp, *sc in next tr, hdc in next tr, dc in next 2 tr, 2 dc in next tr, picot, 2 dc in next tr, dc in each of next 2 tr, hdc in next tr, sc in next tr, 5 sc in next ch-4 sp; rep from * twice more, join in first sc. Fasten off.

**Rnd 9:** Attach D in the 3rd sc of any 5-sc group, ch

4, (2 tr, ch 2, 3 tr) in same sc, ch 5, 3 sc in next picot, ch 5, *(3 tr, ch 2, 3 tr) in 3rd sc of next 5-sc group, ch 5, 3 sc in next picot, ch 5, rep from * 3 times more, join in 4th ch of beg ch-4.

**Rnd 10:** Ch 3, dc in next 2 tr, (2 dc, ch 2, 2 dc) in next ch-sp, dc in next 3 tr, 6 hdc in next ch-5 sp, hdc in next 3 sc, 6 hdc in next ch-5 sp, *dc in next 3 tr, (2 dc, ch 2, 2 dc) in next ch-2 sp, dc in next 3 tr, 6 hdc in next ch-5 sp, hdc in next 3 sc, 6 hdc in next ch-5 sp, rep from * twice more, join 3rd ch of beg ch-3, fasten off.

**Rnd 11:** Attach C in any corner ch-2 sp, ch 4, [dc, ch 1] 5 times in same sp, sk next 2 sts, (sc, ch 3, sc) in next st, [ch 1, sk next 4 sts, {dc, ch 1} 5 times in next st, sk next 4 sts, (sc, ch 3, sc) in next st] twice, ch 1, sk next 2 sts, *[dc, ch 1] 6 times in next corner ch-2 sp, sk next 2 sts, (sc, ch 3, sc) in next st, [ch 1, sk next 4 sts, {dc, ch 1} 5 times in next st, sk next 4 sts, (sc, ch 3, sc) in next st] twice; ch 1, sk next 2 sts, rep from * twice more, join in 3rd ch of beg ch-4. Fasten off.

## SECOND MOTIF

Work same as First Motif through Rnd 10.

**Rnd 11 (joining rnd):** Attach C in any corner ch-2 sp, ch 4 *(counts as first dc and ch-1 sp)*, [dc, ch 1] 5 times in same sp, sk next 2 sts, (sc, ch 3, sc) in next st, [ch 1, sk next 4 sts, {dc, ch 1} 5 times in next st, sk next 4 sts, (sc, ch 3, sc) in next st] twice, ch 1, sk next 2 sts, [dc, ch 1] twice in next corner ch-2 sp, dc in same sp; ch 1, sl st in 3rd ch-1 sp in any corner on adjacent motif, ch 1, [dc, ch 1] 3 times in same sp on working motif, sk next 2 sts, sc in next st, ch 1, sl st in next ch-3 sp on adjacent motif, ch 1, sc in same st on working motif, ch 1, sk next 4 sts, *(dc, ch 1, dc) in next st, sk next ch-1 sp on adjacent motif, [sl st in next ch-1 sp on adjacent motif, (dc, ch 1, dc) in same st on working motif] twice, ch 1, dc in same st, sk next 4 sts, (sc, ch 1, sl st in next ch-1 sp on adjacent motif, ch 1, sc) in next st on working motif**; sk next 4 sts, rep from *, ending at **, sk next 2 sts, [dc, ch 1] twice in next corner ch-2 sp, dc in same sp, ch 1, sl st in 3rd ch-1 sp in corresponding corner on adjacent

motif; ch 1, [dc, ch 1] 3 times in same sp on working motif, sk next 2 sts, (sc, ch 3, sc) in next st, [ch 1, sk next 4 sts, {dc, ch 1} 5 times in next st, sk next 4 sts, (sc, ch 3, sc) in next st] twice, ch 1, sk next 2 sts, [dc, ch 1] 6 times in next corner ch-2 sp; sk next 2 sts, (sc, ch 3, sc) in next st, [ch 1, sk next 4 sts, {dc, ch 1} 5 times in next st, sk next 4 sts, (sc, ch 3, sc) in next st] twice, ch 1, join in 3rd ch of beg ch-4. Fasten off.

## REMAINING MOTIFS

Referring to Assembly Diagram for motif placement, work rem motifs same as Second Motif. Join to adjacent motifs in similar manner making sure all 4-corner joinings are secure. ❧

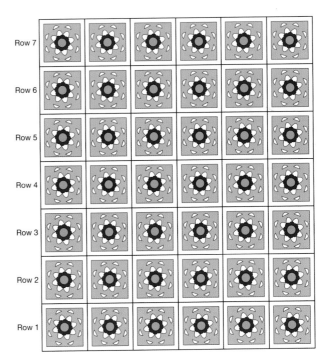

**Roses Are Blue**
Assembly Diagram

# LILY HEXAGONS

Design by Joyce Nordstrom

## FINISHED SIZE
Approximately 46 x 64 inches

## MATERIALS
- TLC Amore medium (worsted) weight yarn (6 oz/290 yds/170g per skein): 6 skeins #3627 light thyme (A), 2 skeins #3103 vanilla (B)
- Size I/9/5.5mm crochet hook or size needed to obtain gauge

## GAUGE
Rnds 1–5 of motif = 8½ inches from point to point
To save time, take time to check gauge.

## SPECIAL STITCHES
For **front post double crochet (fpdc):** Yo, insert hook from front to back around **post** (see Stitch Guide) of st indicated, yo, draw lp through, [yo, draw through 2 lps on hook] twice.

For **cluster (cl):** Keeping last lp of each st on hook, 2 dc in st or sp indicated, yo and draw through all 3 lps on hook.

## PATTERN NOTE
Join with slip stitch unless otherwise stated.

## FIRST MOTIF
## FLOWER CENTER
**Rnd 1 (RS):** With B ch 5, to form ring, ch 3 (counts as hdc and ch-1 sp), [hdc in ring, ch 1] 11 times, join in 2nd ch of beg ch 3. (12 hdc)

**Rnd 2:** Sl st in next ch 1 sp; ch 6 (counts as dc and ch-3 sp), [**fpdc** (see Special Stitches) around next hdc, ch 3, dc in next sp, ch 3] 11 times; fpdc, ch 3, join in 3rd ch of beg ch 6. Fasten off.

## FLOWER BACKGROUND
**Rnd 1 (RS):** Join A with sc to right of dc in any ch-1 sp of Rnd 1 of flower, working behind dc and fpdc of Rnd 2, [ch 5, sk ch-1 sp, sc to right of dc in next ch-1 sp] 5 times, ch 2, join with dc in first sc. (6 ch-5 sps)

**Rnd 2:** Ch 2, dc in sp formed by joining dc, *ch 2, [**cl**, (see Special Stitches) ch 1, cl] in next ch 5 sp (shell), rep from * 4 times more, ch 2, cl in next ch-2 sp, ch 1, join in first dc.

**Rnd 3:** Sl st in next 2 chs of next ch-2 sp, ch 2, dc in same sp (beg cl), *ch 1, shell in ch-1 sp of next shell, ch 1, shell in next ch-2 sp; rep from * 4 times more; ch 1, shell in ch-1 sp of next shell, ch 1, cl in next sp, ch 1, join in top of beg cl (shell). (12 shells)

**Rnd 4:** Ch 2, dc in same sp, *ch 1, (shell, ch 1, cl) in next shell, ch 1, shell in next shell, rep from * 4 times; ch 1, (shell, ch 1, cl) in next shell, ch 1, cl in next ch-1 sp, ch 1, join in top of beg cl.

**Rnd 5:** Ch 2, dc in same sp, *ch 1, shell in next shell, ch 3 (corner), shell in next ch-1 sp; ch 1, shell in next shell; rep from * 4 times more, ch 1, shell in next shell, ch 3, (corner), shell in next ch-1 sp, ch 1, cl in next ch-1 sp, ch 1; join in top of beg cl. Fasten off.

## ADDITIONAL MOTIFS
Work same as First Motif through Rnd 4 of Flower Background.

Referring to Assembly Diagram, join additional motifs in Rnd 5 using One-Side Joining, Two-Side Joining or Three-Side Joining instructions.

## ONE-SIDE JOINING

**Rnd 5:** Ch 2, dc in same sp, ch 1, shell in next shell, ch 1, sl st in ch-3 sp of adjacent motif, ch 1, *cl in next ch-1 sp on working motif, sl st in corresponding ch-1 sp on adjacent motif, cl in same ch-1 sp on working motif, sl st in next ch-1 sp on adjacent motif; rep from * once more, cl in next ch-1 sp, sl st in corresponding ch-1 sp on adjacent motif, cl in same ch-1 sp on working motif, ch 1, sl st in next ch-3 sp on adjacent motif, ch 1, shell in next ch-1 sp on working motif, ch 1, **shell in next ch-1 sp, [ch 1, shell in next shell] twice, ch 3 (corner); rep from ** 3 times more, shell in next ch-1 sp, ch 1, sk next ch-1 sp, cl in next ch-1 sp, ch 1, join in top of beg cl. Fasten off.

## TWO-SIDE JOINING

**Rnd 5:** Ch 2, dc in same sp, ch 1, shell in next shell, ch 1, sl st in ch-3 sp of adjacent motif, ch 1, *cl in next ch-1 sp on working motif, sl st in corresponding ch-1 sp on adjacent motif, cl in same ch-1 sp on working motif, sl st in next ch-1 sp on adjacent motif; rep from * once more, cl in next ch-1 sp, sl st in corresponding ch-1 sp on adjacent motif, cl in same ch-1 sp on working motif, ch 1, sl st in joining on adjacent motifs, ch 1, **cl in next ch-1 sp on working motif, sl st in corresponding ch-1 sp on adjacent motif, cl in same ch-1 sp on working motif, sl st in next ch-1 sp on adjacent motif; rep from ** once more, cl in next ch-1 sp on working motif, sl st in corresponding ch-1 sp on adjacent motif, cl in same ch-1 sp on working motif, ch 1, sl st in ch-3 sp of adjacent motif, ch 1, ***shell in next ch-1 sp on working motif, [ch 1, shell in next shell] twice, ch 3 (corner); rep from *** twice more, shell in next ch-1

sp, ch 1, sk next ch-1 sp, cl in next ch-1 sp, ch 1, join in top of beg cl. Fasten off.

## THREE-SIDE JOINING

**Rnd 5:** Ch 2, dc in same sp, ch 1, shell in next shell, ch 1, sl st in ch-3 sp of adjacent motif, ch 1, *cl in next ch-1 sp on working motif, sl st in corresponding ch-1 sp on adjacent motif, cl in same ch-1 sp on working motif, sl st in next ch-1 sp on adjacent motif; rep from * once more, cl in next ch-1 sp on working motif, sl st in corresponding ch-1 sp on adjacent motif, cl in same ch-1 sp on working motif, [ch 1, sl st in joining on adjacent motifs, ch 1, **cl in next ch-1 sp on working motif, sl st in corresponding ch-1 sp on adjacent motif, cl in same ch-1 sp on working motif, sl st in next ch-1 sp on adjacent motif; rep from ** once more, cl in next ch-1 sp on working motif, sl st in corresponding ch-1 sp on adjacent motif, cl in same ch-1 sp on working motif], rep between [ ] once, ch 1, sl st in ch-3 sp of adjacent motif, ch 1, ***shell in next ch-1 sp on working motif, [ch 1, shell in next shell] 2 times, ch 3; rep from *** once more, shell in next ch-1 sp, ch 1, sk next ch-1 sp, cl in next ch-1 sp, ch 1, join in top of beg cl. Fasten off.

## BORDER

**Rnd 1:** Join B with an sc in ch-3 corner sp indicated on Assembly Diagram, ch 1, sc in same sp, ch 1, [*{sc in top of cl, ch 1} 6 times, (sc, ch 1) twice in next ch-3 corner sp, **{sc in top of cl, ch 1} 6 times, sc in joining, ch 1; rep from ** once, {sc in top of cl, ch 1} 6 times, (sc, ch 1) twice in next corner ch-3 sp, rep from * twice more, {sc in top of cl, ch 1} 6 times, (sc, ch 1) twice in next ch-3 corner sp, ***{sc in top of cl, ch 1} 6 times, (sc, ch 1) twice in next ch-3 corner sp, {sc in top of next cl, ch 1} 6 times, sc in joining, ch 1, rep from *** 6 times, {sc in top of next cl, ch 1} 6 times, (sc, ch 1) twice in next ch-3 corner sp, {sc in top of next cl, ch 1} 6 times], (sc, ch 1) twice in next ch-3 corner sp, rep between [ ] once; join in first sc, changing to A by drawing lp through.

**Rnd 2:** Sl st in next ch-1 sp, ch 2, (dc, ch 1, cl, ch 1) in same sp, [*{cl in next ch-1 sp, ch 1} 7 times, (shell, ch 1) in next ch-1 sp, {cl in next ch-1 sp, ch 1} 6 times, sk next sc and next ch-1 sp, cl in next sc, sk next ch-1 sp, {cl in next ch-1 sp, ch 1} 5 times, sk next sc and next ch-1 sp, cl in next sc, sk next ch-1 sp, {cl in next ch-1 sp, ch 1} 6 times, (cl, ch 1) in next ch-1 sp; rep from * 2 times more, {cl in next ch-1 sp, ch 1} 7 times, (shell, ch 1) in next ch-1 sp, {cl in next ch-1 sp, ch 1} 7 times, (shell, ch 1) in next ch-1 sp, **{cl in next ch-1 sp, ch 1} 6 times, sk next sc and next ch-1 sp, cl in next sc, sk next ch-1 sp, {cl in next ch-1 sp, ch 1} 6 times, (shell, ch 1) in next ch-1 sp, rep from ** 6 times more, {cl in next ch-1 sp, ch 1} 7 times], (shell, ch 1) in next ch-1 sp, rep between [ ] once; join in first dc. Fasten off.

**Rnd 3:** Join B in ch-1 sp of any shell, working from left to right, [sc, ch 1] in each ch-1 sp around, working [sc, ch 2, sc] in each shell. Fasten off and weave in all ends. ❧

Start border here

First Row · Second Row · Third Row · Fourth Row · Fifth Row · Sixth Row · Seventh Row

**Lily Hexagons**
Assembly Diagram

# PASSION FOR PURPLE

Design by Carol Alexander

## FINISHED SIZE
Approximately 48 x 60 inches

## MATERIALS
- Red Heart Super Saver medium (worsted) weight yarn (8 oz/452 yds/225g per skein): 3 skeins #358 lavender (A), 4 skeins #316 soft white (B), 1 skein each #320 cornmeal (C) and #389 hunter green (E)
- Red Heart Classic medium (worsted) weight yarn (3½ oz/198 yds/99g per skein): 4 skeins #683 light seafoam (D)
- Size G/6/4mm crochet hook or size needed to obtain gauge

## GAUGE
Rnds 1–6 of motif = 7 x 8 inches at widest point
To save time, take time to check gauge.

## SPECIAL STITCHES
For **picot:** Ch 4, sl st in 4th ch from hook.
For **single crochet picot (sc picot):** Ch 2, sc around post *(see Stitch Guide)* of last tr made.
For **V-stitch (V-st):** (Dc, ch 1, dc) in st or sp indicated.
For **joining V-st:** (Dc, sl st in ch-1 sp of corresponding V-st on motif indicated, dc) in st indicated on working motif.

## PATTERN NOTE
Join with a slip stitch unless otherwise stated.

## FIRST ROW
### FIRST MOTIF
**Rnd 1 (RS):** With C, ch 4, join to form ring, ch 1, [sc in ring, **picot** *(see Special Stitches)*] 8 times, join in **front lp** only of first sc. Fasten off. *(8 sc and 8 picots)*

**Rnd 2:** With WS of Rnd 1 facing, attach A in **back lp** of any sc, working behind picots, ch 3 *(counts as first dc of bottom row of petal)*, 4 dc in same st, turn, ch 3 *(counts as first dc of top row of petal)*, dc in each of next 4 dc, turn, ch 2, *working behind petal just made, 5 dc in **back lp** of next sc on Rnd 1, turn, ch 3 *(counts as dc)*, dc in each of next 4 dc, turn, ch 2; rep from * 6 times more, join in 3rd ch of beg ch-3. Fasten off. *(8 petals)*
**Note:** *WS of Rnd 1 now becomes the RS of flower.*

## FIRST TWO LEAVES
With RS of flower facing, attach E in **front lp** of first ch of ch-2 sp behind any flower petal of Rnd 2; working behind petal, ch 4, (tr, **sc picot** *{see Special Stitches}*, tr) in **front lp** of same ch, ch 4, sl st in **front lp** of same ch, catching lp on upper back of post of 2nd dc made on top row of same petal, ch 4, (tr, sc picot, tr) in **front lp** of same ch, catching lp on upper back of post of last dc made on first row of same petal, (ch 4, sl st) in **front lp** of same ch. Fasten off. *(2 leaves)*

## SECOND TWO LEAVES
Sk next 3 ch-2 sps of Rnd 2, attach E in **front lp** of first ch of next ch-2, make 2 leaves as for first 2 leaves in **front lp** of ch.

**Rnd 3:** Attach B in ch-2 sp of Rnd 2 behind first flower petal to left of any leaf pair, ch 3 *(counts as first dc)*, 3 dc in same sp, catching lp on upper back of post of 2nd dc made on top row of same petal with 3rd dc, 2 dc in same sp, catching lp on upper back of last dc made on first row of same petal with 2nd dc, [4 dc in next ch-2 sp, catching lp on upper back of post of 2nd dc made on top row of next flower petal with 4th dc, 2 dc in same sp, catching

lp on upper back of post of last dc made on first row of same petal with 2nd of these dc] twice, working behind leaves in next ch-2, 3 dc in **back lp** of same ch where leaves were worked, 3 dc in 2nd ch of ch-2 sp, rep between [ ] 3 times, working behind leaves in next ch-2 sp, 3 dc in back lp of same ch where leaves were worked, 3 dc in 2nd ch of ch-2 sp; join in 3rd ch of beg ch-3. *(48 sts)*

**Note:** *Smooth flower petals evenly, making sure leaves are flat behind flower petals.*

**Rnd 4:** Ch 4 *(counts as tr)*, *dc in each of next 4 sts, hdc in each of next 4 sts, 3 hdc in next st, hdc in each of next 4 sts, dc in each of next 4 sts, tr in each of next 2 sts, tr in next st, catching lp on upper back of first leaf of leaf pair, 3 tr in next st, tr in next st, catching lp on upper back of 2nd leaf of leaf pair**, tr in each of next 2 sts, rep from * once more, ending at **, tr in next st, join in 4th ch of beg ch-4.

**Rnd 5:** Ch 3 *(counts as first dc)*, *dc in each of next 9 sts, (2 dc, ch 1, 2 dc) in next st *(center hdc of 3-hdc group)*, dc in each of next 11 sts, tr in each of next 2 sts, (2 tr, ch 2, 2 tr) in next st *(center tr of 3-tr group)*, tr in each of next 2 sts**, dc in each of next 2 sts, rep from * once, ending at **, dc in next st, join in 3rd ch of beg ch-3. Fasten off.

**Note:** *Work Rnd 6 loosely to keep edges flat.*

**Rnd 6:** Attach D in ch-2 sp at either tip of diamond motif, ch 3, (dc, ch 3, 2 dc) in same sp, *ch 1, sk 2 sts, sl st in next st, [ch 1, sk 1 st, **V-st** *(see Special Stitches)* in next st, ch 1, sk 1 st, sl st in next st] 3 times, ch 1, sk next 2 sts**, (2 dc, ch 3, 2 dc) in next corner sp, rep from * 3 times, ending last rep at **, join in 3rd ch of beg ch-3. Fasten off.

## SECOND ROW
## FIRST MOTIF

Work same as First Motif on First Row.

## SECOND MOTIF

Work same as Rnds 1–5 of First Motif on First Row.

**Rnd 6 (joining rnd):** Attach D in ch-2 sp at either tip of diamond motif, ch 3, 2 dc in corner sp, ch 1, with WS of previous motif facing WS of working motif, sl st in corresponding corner ch-3 sp on previous motif, ch 1, 2 dc in same sp on working motif, [ch 1, sk next 2 sts, sl st in next st, {ch 1, sk 1 st, **joining V-st** *(see Special Stitches)* in next st, ch 1, sk next st, sl st in next st} 3 times, ch 1, sk next 2 sts, 2 dc in next corner st, ch 1], sl st in corresponding corner ch-3 sp on previous motif and adjacent motif on previous row at same time, ch 1, 2 dc in same st on working motif, rep between [ ] once, sl st in corresponding corner ch-3 sp on previous motif, 2 dc in same sp on working motif, *ch 1, sk 2 sts, sl st in next st, [ch 1, sk 1 st, V-st in next st, ch 1, sk 1 st, sl st in next st] 3 times, ch 1, sk next 2 sts**, (2 dc, ch 3, 2 dc) in next corner sp, rep from * once ending at **, join in 3rd ch of beg ch-3.

Continued on page 25

**Passion for Purple**
Assembly Diagram

# SPRING FLORAL

Design by Katherine Eng

## FINISHED SIZE
Approximately 44 x 58 inches

## MATERIALS
- Red Heart Super Saver medium (worsted) weight yarn (6 oz/290 yds/170g per skein): 1 skein each #724 baby pink (A) and #329 eggnog (B)
- Red Heart Hokey Pokey medium (worsted) weight yarn (6 oz/290 yds/170g per skein): 8 skeins #7220 spearmint (C), 2 skeins each #7107 bubblegum (D) and #7109 sunshine (E)
- Size H/8/5mm crochet hook or size needed to obtain gauge

## GAUGE
Rnds 1–9 of motif = 5½ inches square
To save time, take time to check gauge.

## SPECIAL STITCHES
For **joining ch-2 sp:** Ch 2, drop lp from hook, insert hook in corresponding ch-4 sp on adjacent motif, pull dropped lp through, ch 2.

For **joining ch-1 sp:** Ch 1, drop lp from hook, insert hook in corresponding ch-4 sp on adjacent motif, pull dropped lp through, ch 1.

## PATTERN NOTE
Join with a slip stitch unless otherwise stated.

## FIRST MOTIF
**Rnd 1:** With E, ch 6, join to form ring, ch 1, [sc in ring, ch 2] 8 times, join in first sc. Fasten off.

**Rnd 2:** Working behind Rnd 1, attach D with sc over beg ch between any 2 sc of Rnd 1, ch 3, [sc over beg ch between same sc and next sc, ch 3] 7 times, join in first sc.

**Rnd 3:** Ch 1, sc in same sc, (hdc, dc, tr, ch 1, dc, hdc) in next ch-3 sp *(petal)*, [sc in sc, (hdc, dc, tr, ch 1, dc, hdc) in next ch 3 sp *(petal)*] 7 times, join in first sc. Fasten off. *(8 petals)*

**Rnd 4:** Working behind petals on rnd 3, attach C with sc in any sc, ch 3, [sc in next sc, ch 3] 7 times, join in first sc.

**Rnd 5:** Ch 1, (sc, ch 1, sc) in same sp, ch 1, (sc, ch 1, sc) in next ch-3 sp, *(sc, ch 1, sc) in next sc, (sc, ch 1, sc) in next ch-3 sp; rep from * 6 times more times, join in first sc.

**Rnd 6:** Sl st in next ch-1 sp, ch 1, sc in same sp, [ch 1, sc in next ch 2 sp] twice, ch 1, (3 dc, ch 2, 3 dc) in next ch 2 sp, *[ch 1, sc in next ch-2 sp] 3 times, ch 1, (3 dc, ch 2, 3 dc) in next ch-2 sp; rep from * twice more, ch 1, join in first sc.

**Rnd 7:** Ch 1, sc in same sc, in each st and in each ch-1 sp to corner ch-2 sp, (sc, ch 2, sc) in next ch-2 sp, *sc in each st and each ch-1 sp to next corner ch-2 sp, (sc, ch 2, sc) in corner ch-2 sp; rep from * twice more, sc in each st to first sc, join in first sc. Fasten off.

**Rnd 8:** Attach E with sc in 2nd sc to left of any corner ch-2 sp, ch 1, sc in same sc, [ch 1, sk next sc, sc in next sc] 6 times, ch 1, sk next sc, (sc, ch 2, sc) in corner ch-2 sp, *[ch 1, sk next sc, sc in next sc] 7 times, ch 1, sk next sc, (sc, ch 2, sc) in corner ch-2 sp; rep from * twice more, ch 1, join in first sc. Fasten off.

**Rnd 9:** Attach C with sc in 2nd sc to left of any corner ch-2 sp, ch 1, sc in same sc, *[ch 1, (sc, ch 1, sc) in next sc, ch 1, sc in next sc] 3 times, ch 1, (sc, ch 1, sc) in next sc, (sc, ch 4, sc) in corner ch-2 sp, (sc, ch 2, sc) in next sc, ch 1, ** sc in next sc, *rep from * 3 times more, ending last rep at **, join in first sc. Fasten off.

## SECOND MOTIF

Referring to Assembly Diagram for color and placement, work same as Rnds 1–8, of First Motif.

**Rnd 9 (joining rnd):** Attach C with an sc in 2nd sc to left of any corner ch-2 sp, ch 1, sc in same sc, *[ch 1, (sc, ch 1, sc) in next sc, ch 1, sc in next sc] 3 times, ch 1, (sc, ch 1, sc) in next sc, [2 sc, **joining ch-2 sp** (see Special Stitches), sc] in next corner ch-2 sp, ch 1, [sc, **joining ch-1 sp** (see Special Stitches), sc] in next sc, ch 1, sc in next sc, ch 1] 4 times, (sc, joining ch-1 sp, sc) in next sc, ch 1, (sc, joining ch-2 sp, sc) in next corner ch-2 sp, *[ch 1, (sc, ch 1, sc) in next sc, ch 1, sc in next sc] 4 times, ch 1, (sc, ch 1, sc) in next sc, ch 1, (sc, ch 4, sc) in next corner ch-4 sp, rep from * once more, ch 1, (sc, ch 1, sc) in next sc, ch 1, join in first sc. Fasten off.

## REMAINING MOTIFS

Referring to Assembly Diagram for color and placement, work rem motifs same as for Second Motif, joining to adjacent motifs in similar manner and making sure all 4-corner joinings are secure.

## BORDER

**Note:** For **dec**, yo, draw up lp in each of next 2 ch-4 sp, yo and draw through 3 lps on hook, yo and draw through 2 lps on hook.

**Rnd 1:** Hold with RS facing and one short edge at top, attach C in first ch-2 sp to left of upper right-hand corner ch-4 sp, ch 1, sc in same sp, [ch 3, sc in next ch-2 sp] 4 times, ch 3, *[**dec** (see note), (ch 3, sc in next ch-2 sp) 5 times, ch 3] to next corner, (sc, ch 3, sc) in corner ch-4 sp, (ch 3, sc in next ch-2 sp) 5 times, ch 3; rep from * once more, [dec, (ch 3, sc in next ch-2 sp) 5 times, ch 3] to next corner, (sc, ch 3, sc) in corner ch-4 sp, ch 3, join.

**Rnd 2:** Sl st in next ch-3 sp, ch 1, sc in same sp, *[3 dc in next st, sc in next ch-3 sp] to next corner, 5 dc in corner ch-3 sp; rep from * 3 times more, sc in next ch-3 sp, 3 dc in next st, join in first sc.

**Rnd 3:** Sl st in next 2 dc, ch 1, (sc, ch 2, sc) in same dc, ch 1, sl st in next sc, *[(sc, ch 2, sc) in 2nd dc of next 3-dc group, sl st in next sc] to next corner, ch 2, sk next dc, (sc, ch 2, sc) in next dc, (sc, ch 3, sc) in next dc, (sc, ch 2, sc) in next dc, ch 2, sk next dc, sl st in next sc; rep from * 3 times more, (sc, ch 2, sc) in 2nd dc of next 3-dc group, join in joining sl st. Fasten off and weave in all ends. 🐦

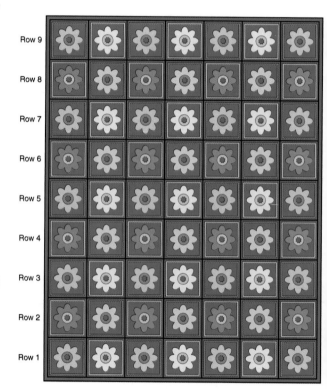

**Spring Floral**
Assembly Diagram

# DESERT FLOWERS

Design by Brenda Stratton

## FINISHED SIZE
Approximately 48 x 64 inches

## MATERIALS
- Red Heart Super Saver medium (worsted) weight yarn (8 oz/452 yds/225g per skein): 4 skeins #316 soft white (E), 3 skeins #631 light sage (D), 2 skeins #633 dark sage (C), 1 skein #320 cornmeal (A)
- Red Heart Classic medium (worsted) weight yarn (3½ oz/198 yds/99g per skein): 2 skeins #848 skipper blue (B), 1 skein each #730 grenadine (F) and #252 medium coral (G)
- Red Heart Kids medium (worsted) weight yarn (5 oz/302 yds/140g per skein): 1 skein #2360 orchid (H)
- Size G/6/4mm crochet hook (for flowers only)
- Size H/8/5mm crochet hook or size needed to obtain gauge

## GAUGE
Rnds 1–12 of motif = 8 inches square
To save time, take time to check gauge.

## SPECIAL STITCHES
For **treble cluster (tr cl):** *(Yo twice, pull up lp in st or sp indicated, [yo, draw through 2 lps] twice, rep from * once more, yo and draw through all 3 lps on hook.
For **long double crochet (long dc):** (Yo, pull up lp in st or sp indicated on rnd below to height of working row, [yo, draw through 2 lps] twice.

## PATTERN NOTES
Join with a slip stitch unless otherwise stated.

## FIRST MOTIF
**Rnd 1 (flower center):** With smaller hook and A, ch 4, join to form ring, ch 2 *(counts as hdc)*, 11 hdc in ring, join in **back lp** of 2nd ch of beg ch-2. Fasten off. *(12 hdc)*

**Rnd 2:** Attach B in same ch as joining, ch 1, sc in same ch, working in **back lps** only, sc in each hdc, join in **front lp** of first sc.

**Rnd 3:** Working in **front lps** only, *ch 3, (dc, ch 2, sl st in top of dc just worked, ch 3, sl st) in same lp *(petal),* sk next sc, sl st in next lp; rep from * 4 times more; ch 3, (dc, ch 2, sl st in top of dc just worked, ch 3, sl st) in same lp *(petal),* join in joining sl st. *(6 petals)*

**Rnd 4:** Sl st in **back lp** of first skipped sc on Rnd 2; *ch 3, (dc, ch 2, sl st in top of dc just worked, ch 3, sl st) in same lp *(petal),* sl st in back lp of next skipped sc; rep from * 4 times more; ch 3, (dc, ch 2, sl st in top of dc just worked, ch 3, sl st) in same lp (petal), join in joining sl st. *(6 petals)*

**Rnd 5:** Ch 4, sk next petal, sl st in base of next petal, ch 4, sk next petal, sl st in sp between next 2 petals, ch 4, sk next petal, sl st in base of next petal, ch 4, join in joining sl st. Fasten off. *(4 ch-4 lps)*

**Rnd 6 (leaves):** With larger hook, attach C in any ch-4 lp, *[ch 4, **tr cl** *(see Special Stitches),* ch 2, sl st in top of tr cl, ch 4, sl st in same lp *(petal)*] twice, sl st in next ch-4 lp; rep from * twice more, [ch 4, tr cl, ch 2, sl st in top of tr cl, ch 4, sl st in same lp *(petal)*] twice, join in joining sl st. *(8 leaves)*

**Rnd 7:** Ch 3, *sl st between next 2 leaves, ch 3, rep from * around, join in joining sl st. Fasten off. *(8 ch-3 lps)*

**Rnd 8:** Attach D in any ch-3 sp, ch 3 *(counts as a dc),* 3 dc in same lp, *4 dc in next ch-3 sp; rep from * around, join in 3rd ch of beg ch-3. *(32 dc)*

**Rnd 9 (anchor row):** Ch 3, dc in next dc, *yo, insert hook through top of tr cl on corresponding leaf and

in next dc, yo, draw lp through both sts, [yo, draw through 2 lps on hook] twice, dc in same dc and in next 3 dc; rep from * 6 times more, yo, insert hook through top of tr cl on corresponding leaf and in next dc, yo, draw lp through both sts, [yo, draw through 2 lps on hook] twice, dc in same dc and in next dc, join in 3rd ch of beg ch-3. Fasten off.

**Rnd 10:** Attach E in same ch as joining, ch 4 *(counts as dc and ch-1 sp)*, (dc, ch 3, dc, ch 1, dc) in same st *(corner)*, *ch 2, sk next 2 dc, sc in next 5 dc, ch 2, sk next 2 dc, (dc, ch 1, dc, ch 3, ch 1, dc) in next dc *(corner)*; rep from * twice more, ch 2, sk next 2 dc, sc in next 5 dc, ch 2, sk next 2 dc, join in 3rd ch of beg ch-4.

**Rnd 11:** Sl st in next ch-1 sp, ch 4, *(dc, ch 3, dc) in next corner ch-3 sp, ch 1, dc in next ch-1 sp, ch 1, dc in next ch-2 sp, ch 1, [dc in next sc, ch 1, sk next sc] twice, dc in next sc, ch 1, dc in next ch-2 sp, ch 1, dc in next ch-1 sp, ch 1; rep from * twice more, (dc, ch 3, dc) in next corner ch-3 sp, ch 1, dc in next ch-1 sp, ch 1, dc in next ch-2 sp, ch 1, [dc in next sc, ch 1, sk next sc] twice, dc in next sc, ch 1, dc in next ch-2 sp, ch 1, join in 3rd ch of beg ch-4.

**Rnd 12:** Sl st in next ch-1 sp, ch 3, dc in same sp, *(2 dc, ch 5, 2 dc) in next corner ch-3 sp, 2 dc in each of next 8 ch-1 sps; rep from * twice more; (2 dc, ch 5, 2 dc) in next corner ch-3 sp, 2 dc in each of next 7 ch-1 sps, join in 3rd ch of beg ch-3. Fasten off.

**Rnd 13:** Attach D in any ch-5 corner sp, ch 3, 6 dc in same sp, *sk next dc, [sc in next dc, sk next 2 dc, 5 dc in next dc; sk next 2 dc] twice; sc in next dc, sk next 2 dc, 5 dc in next dc, sk next dc, sc in next dc, sk next dc, 7 dc in next corner ch-5 sp; rep from * twice more, sk next dc, [sc in next dc, sk next 2 dc, 5 dc in next dc. sk next 2 dc] twice, sc in next dc, sk next 2 dc, 5 dc in next dc, sk next dc, sc in next dc, sk next dc, join in 3rd ch of beg ch-3. Fasten off.

**Rnd 14:** Attach E in 4th dc of any corner, ch 1, (sc, ch 5, sc) in same, *(sc, ch 1, sc) in next dc, [**long dc** *(see Special Stitches)*, ch 3, long dc] in same dc on Rnd 12 as next sc on previous rnd worked; (sc, ch 1, sc) in 3rd dc of next 5-dc group, [(long dc, ch 3, long

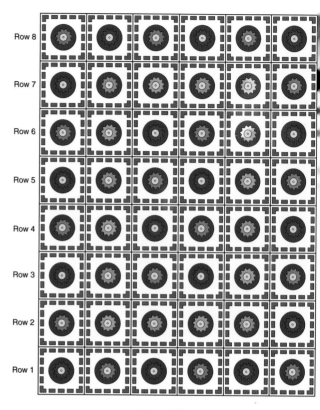

**Desert Flowers**
Assembly Diagram

dc) in same dc on Rnd 12 as next sc on previous rnd worked, (sc, ch 1, sc) in 3rd dc of next 5-dc group] twice; (long dc, ch 3, long dc) in same dc on Rnd 12 as next sc on previous rnd worked, sk next 2 dc, (sc, ch 1, sc) in next dc, (sc, ch 5, sc) in next dc; rep from * twice more, (sc, ch 1, sc) in next dc, [(long dc, ch 3, long dc) in same dc on Rnd 12 as next sc on previous rnd worked, (sc, ch 1, sc) in 3rd dc of next 5-dc group] 3 times, (long dc, ch 3, long dc) in same dc on Rnd 12 as next sc on previous rnd worked, sk next 2 dc, (sc, ch 1, sc) in next dc, join in first sc. Fasten off.

## SECOND MOTIF

Referring to Assembly Diagram for flower color, work same as Rnds 1–13 of First Motif.

**Rnd 14:** Attach E in 4th dc of any corner, ch 1, (sc, ch 5, sc) in same dc, (sc, ch 1, sc) in next dc, [(long dc, ch 3, long dc) in same dc on Rnd 12 as next sc on previous rnd worked, (sc, ch 1, sc) in 3rd dc of next 5-dc group] 3 times; (long dc, ch 3, long dc) in same dc on Rnd 12 as next sc on previous rnd worked, sk next 2 dc, (sc, ch 1, sc) in next dc, sc in next dc, ch 2, sl st in adjacent corner ch-5 sp on adjacent motif, ch 2, sc in same dc on working motif, (sc, ch 1, sc) in next dc, [long dc in same dc on Rnd 12 as next sc on previous rnd worked, ch 1, sl st in next ch-3 sp on completed motif, ch 1, long dc in same dc on Rnd 12, (sc, ch 1, sc) in 3rd dc of next 5-dc group] 3 times, long dc in same dc on Rnd 12 as next sc on previous rnd worked, ch 1, sl st in next ch-3 sp on adjacent motif, ch 1, long dc in same dc on Rnd 12, sk next 2 dc, (sc, ch 1, sc) in next dc, sc in next dc, ch 2, sl st in next corner ch-5 sp on completed motif, ch 2, sc in same dc on working motif, (sc, ch 1, sc) in next dc, [(long dc, ch 3, long dc) in same dc on Rnd 12 as next sc on previous rnd worked, (sc, ch 1, sc) in 3rd dc of next 5-dc group] 3 times, (long dc, ch 3, long dc) in same dc on Rnd 12 as next sc on previous rnd worked; sk next 2 dc, (sc, ch 1, sc) in next dc, (sc, ch 5, sc) in next dc, (sc, ch 1, sc) in next dc, [(long dc, ch 3, long dc) in same dc on Rnd 12 as next sc on previous rnd worked, (sc, ch 1, sc) in 3rd dc of next 5-dc group] 3 times, (long dc, ch 3, long dc) in same dc on Rnd 12 as next sc on previous rnd worked, sk next 2 dc, (sc, ch 1, sc) in next dc, join in first sc. Fasten off.

### REMAINING MOTIFS

Referring to Assembly Diagram for flower color and placement, work rem motifs same as for Second Motif, joining to adjacent motifs in similar manner and making sure all 4-corner joinings are secure. 🌿

# PASSION FOR PURPLE Continued from page 18

### LAST MOTIF

Work same as Rnds 1–5 of First Motif on First Row.

**Rnd 6 (joining rnd):** Attach D in ch-2 sp at either tip of diamond motif, ch 3, (dc, ch 3, 2 dc) in same sp, *[ch 1, sk 2 sts, sl st in next st, {ch 1, sk 1 st, V-st in next st, ch 1, sk 1 st, sl st in next st} 3 times, ch 1, sk next 2 sts] **, (2 dc, ch 3, 2 dc) in next corner sp, rep between [ ] once, 2 dc in corner sp, ch 1, with WS of previous motif facing WS of working motif, sl st in corresponding corner ch-3 sp, ch 1, 2 dc in same sp on working motif, ch 1, sk next 2 sts, sl st in next st, [ch 1, sk 1 st, joining V-st in next st, ch 1, sk 1 st, sl st in next st] 3 times, ch 1, sk next 2 sts, 2 dc in next corner st, ch 1, sl st in corresponding corner ch-3 sp on previous motif, ch 1, 2 dc in same st on 2nd motif, rep from * once ending at **, join in 3rd ch of beg ch-3.

### REMAINING ROWS

Referring to Assembly Diagram on page 18 for motif placement, work rem motifs joining to adjacent motifs in similar manner and joining corners to previously joined corners with a sl st into center of previous joining(s). 🌿

# FANTASY FLOWERS

These designs range from vibrant to soft and feminine in feel. You'll enjoy the color and bright optimism they bring to your surroundings.

# SWEET IMAGINATION

Design by Bonnie Pierce

## FINISHED SIZE
Approximately 35 x 49 inches

## MATERIALS
- Super Saver medium (worsted) weight yarn
  (8 oz/452 yds/226g per skein): 3 skeins
  #313 aran (C), 2 skeins #661 frosty green (D),
  1 skein each #358 lavender (A) and #347
  light periwinkle (B)
- Size H/8/5mm or size needed to obtain gauge

## GAUGE
Rnds 1–10 of motif = 7 inches square
To save time, take time to check gauge.

## SPECIAL STITCHES
For **front post single crochet (fpsc):** Insert hook from front to back around **post** (see Stitch Guide) of st indicated, yo, and pull up a lp even with last st worked and complete as sc.

For **front post half double crochet (fphdc):** Yo, insert hook front to back around **post** (see Stitch Guide) of st indicated, yo and pull up a lp even with last st worked and complete as hdc.

For **front post double crochet (fpdc):** Yo, insert hook front to back around **post** (see Stitch Guide) of st indicated, yo and pull up lp even with last st worked and complete as dc.

For **front post treble crochet (fptr):** Yo twice, insert hook from front to back around **post** (see Stitch Guide) of st indicated, yo and pull up lp even with last st worked and complete as a tr.

For **double treble crochet (dtr):** Yo 3 times, insert

hook and pull up lp, (yo, draw through 2 lps on hook) 3 times.

For **pearl stitch roll stitch (pearl roll st):** Drop C, with A yo 5 times, drop A, insert hook in st indicated, with C, yo, draw lp through, yo and draw through all 7 lps on hook.

## PATTERN NOTE
Join with slip stitch unless otherwise stated.

## FIRST ROW
### FIRST MOTIF
**Rnd 1:** With A, ch 5, (dc, ch 2) 7 times in 5th ch from hook, join with in 3rd ch of beg ch-5. Fasten off.

**Rnd 2:** Attach B with an sc over post of any sc, [**fphdc** (see Special Stitches), {**fpdc** (see Special Stitches)} twice, **fptr** (see Special Stitches)] over same post (petal made), *[**fpsc** (see Special Stitches), fphdc, (fpdc) twice, fptr] over post of next dc (petal made), rep from 6 times more, join with in first sc. (8 petals)

**Rnd 3:** Ch 1, sc in same st, hdc in next fphdc, dc in next fpdc, hdc in next fpdc, sc in next fptr, *sc in next fpsc, hdc in next fphdc, dc in next fpdc, hdc in next fpdc, sc in next fptr); rep from * 6 times more, join in first sc. Fasten off and weave in ends.

**Rnd 4:** Working behind petals, join C with sc in any unused ch-2 sp of Rnd 1, (sc, hdc, dc, hdc, sc) in next ch-2 sp, *sc in next ch-1 sp, (sc, hdc, dc, hdc, sc) in next ch-2 sp; rep from * twice more, join in first sc.

**Rnd 5:** Ch 3, dc in same sc and in next 2 sts,*(2 dc, ch 2, 2 dc) in next dc (corner), dc in next 2 sts, 2 dc

in next sc, dc in next 2 sts, rep from * twice more, dc in next 2 sts, join in 3rd ch of beg ch-3. Fasten off.

**Rnd 6:** Attach D with in st before ch-2 corner sp, ch 1, sc in same sp, *working over Rnd 3, **dtr** *(see Special Stitches)* between petals, sc in ch-2 corner sp on working row, working over Rnd 3, dtr between petals, sc in next 10 sts on working row; rep from * twice more, working over Rnd 3, dtr between petals, sc in ch-2 corner sp on working row, working over rnd 3, dtr between petals, sc in next 9 sts on working row; join with in first sc.

**Rnd 7:** Ch 3, dc in next dtr,* (2 dc, ch 2, 2 dc) in corner sc, dc in next 12 sts; rep from * twice more, (2 dc, ch 2, 2 dc) in corner sc, dc in next 10 st, join in 3rd ch of beg ch-3. Fasten off.

**Rnd 8:** Join C with sc in any ch-2 corner sp, 2 sc in same sp, sc in next 16 sts, *3 sc in ch-2 corner sp, sc in next 16 sts; rep from * twice more, join in first sc.

**Rnd 9:** Ch 1, sc in same sc, *3 sc in next sc, sc in next sc, [**pearl roll st** *(see Special Stitches)* in next st with A, sc in next 2 sc with C] 5 times, pearl roll st with A in next sc, sc with C in next sc, rep from * twice more, 3 sc in next sc, sc in next sc, [pearl roll st in next st with A, sc in next 2 sc with C] 5 times, pearl roll st with A in next sc; join with C in first sc. Fasten off A. *(24 pearl roll sts)*

**Rnd 10:** Ch 1, sc in same st and next st, *3 sc in next sc, sc in next 20 sts, rep from * twice more, 3 sc in next sc, sc in next 18 sts, join with sl st in first sc. Fasten off.

## SECOND MOTIF

Work same as First Motif.

## MOTIF JOINING

To **join motifs:** Referring to Assembly Diagram for placement, hold 2 motifs with WS tog, join C through first sc of both motifs at same time. Working through sc of last rnd of both motifs at same time sl st across one side.

To **join rows:** Hold 2 rows with WS tog, working through sc of last rnd of both motifs at same time sl st across row making sure all 4-corner joinings are secure.

## BORDER

**Rnd 1:** Join C with sc in any outer corner, 2 sc in same sc, sc in each st to next outer corner, *3 sc in corner sc, sc in each st to next corner; rep from * 3 times more; join in first sc.

**Rnd 2:** Sc in each sc, working 3 sc in each corner sc; join in first sc.

Fasten off and weave in ends. 🍃

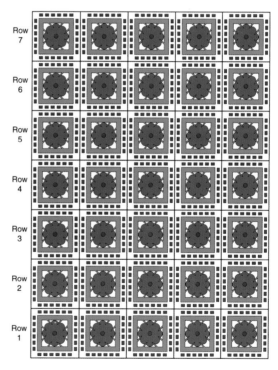

**Sweet Imagination**
Assembly Diagram

# PURE PLEASURE

Design by Carol Alexander

## FINISHED SIZE
Approximately 48 x 64 inches

## MATERIALS
- Super Saver medium (worsted) weight yarn (8 oz/452 yds/225g per skein): 5 skeins #316 soft white (B), 3 skeins #347 light periwinkle (A)
- Super Saver medium (worsted) weight yarn (6 oz/348 yds/170g per skein): #310 Monet print (C)
- Size G/6/4mm crochet hook or size needed to obtain gauge

## GAUGE
Rnds 1–8 of motif = 8 inches square
To save time, take time to check gauge.

## SPECIAL STITCHES
For **beginning popcorn (beg pc):** Ch 3, work 3 dc in same place, drop lp from hook, insert hook from front to back on 3rd ch of beg ch-3, pull dropped lp through.

For **popcorn (pc):** Work 4 dc in place indicated, drop lp from hook, insert hook from front to back in top of first dc, pull dropped lp through.

For **beginning treble crochet cluster (beg tr cl):** Ch 4, holding back last lp of each tr on hook, work 2 tr in same place as ch-4, yo, draw through all 3 lps on hook.

For **treble crochet cluster (tr cl):** Holding back last lp of each tr on hook, work 3 tr in place indicated, yo, draw through all 4 lps on hook.

For **Puff stitch (puff st):** [Yo, insert hook around post *(see Stitch Guide)* of st indicated, yo, pull up lp approximately ½ inch long] 4 times, yo, draw through all 9 lps on hook.

## PATTERN NOTE
Join with a slip stitch unless otherwise stated.

## FIRST MOTIF
**Rnd 1:** With A, ch 5, join to form ring, ch 2 *(counts as first hdc),* 19 hdc in ring, join in 2nd ch of beg ch-2. Fasten off. *(20 hdc)*

**Rnd 2:** Attach B in joining sl st of previous rnd, ch 3 *(counts as hdc and ch-1 sp),* [hdc in next st, ch 1] 19 times, join in 2nd ch of beg ch-3. *(20 hdc and 20 ch-1 sps)*

**Rnd 3:** Sl st in first ch-1 sp, **beg pc** *(see Special Stitches)* in same sp, ch 1, [pc *(see Special Stitches)* in next ch-1 sp, ch 1] 19 times, join in top of beg pc. Fasten off. *(20 pcs and 20 ch-1 sps)*

Continued on page 41

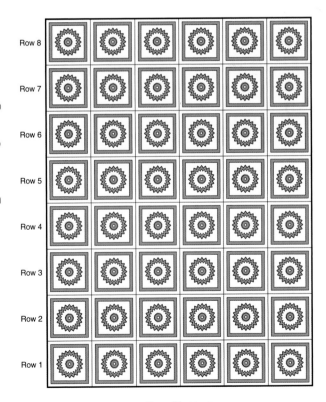

**Pure Pleasure**
Assembly Diagram

# VIOLET VISION

Design by Bonnie Pierce

## FINISHED SIZE
Approximately 40 x 50 inches

## MATERIALS
- Red Heart Super Saver medium (worsted) weight yarn (8 oz/452 yds/226g per skein): 2 skeins each #356 amethyst (A) and #311 white (C), 1 skein each #661 frosty green (B) and #358 lavender (D)
- Size H/8/5mm crochet hook or size needed to obtain gauge

## GAUGE
Rnds 1–8 of motif = 7 inches across
To save time, take time to check gauge.

## SPECIAL STITCHES
For **4-double crochet cluster (4-dc cl):** Keeping last lp of each dc on hook, work 4 dc in same sp or st, yo and draw through all 5 lps on hook.
For **Roll stitch (roll st):** Yo 10 times loosely and evenly, insert hook in st indicated, draw up lp, yo and draw through all 12 lps on hook, ch 1.

## PATTERN NOTE
Join with slip stitch unless otherwise stated.

## FIRST ROW
## FIRST MOTIF
**Rnd 1:** With A, ch 1, sc in ch, ch 2, [**4-dc cl** (see Special Stitches), ch 2, sc, ch 2] 3 times in same ch, 4-dc cl in same ch, ch 2, join in first sc. Draw beg lp closed.
**Rnd 2:** Ch 1, sc in same sc, [ch 5, sc in next sc] 3 times, ch 5, join in first sc. Fasten off.
**Rnd 3:** Attach B in any ch-5 sp, ch 4, (6 dc, tr) in same sp, ch 2, *(tr, 6 dc, tr) in next ch-5 sp,

ch 2; rep from * twice more, join in 4th ch of beg ch-4 changing to C by drawing lp through. Fasten off B.
**Rnd 4:** Ch 1, sc in same ch and in next 7 sts, ch 4 for corner, [sc in next 8 sts, ch 4] 3 times, join in first sc.
**Rnd 5:** Ch 1, sc in same st and next 7 sts, ch 5, [sc in next 8 sts, ch 5] 3 times, join in first sc changing to D by drawing lp through. Fasten off C.
**Rnd 6:** Ch 3, dc in next 7 sts, (5 roll sts) in next ch-5 sp, *dc in next 8 st, (5 roll sts) in next ch-5 sp, rep from twice more, join in 3rd ch of beg ch-3. Fasten off.
**Rnd 7:** Attach A with sl st in sp between first and 2nd roll st of any 5-roll st group, ch 2 (counts as hdc), 2 dc in next sp, ch 2, 2 dc in next sp, hdc in next sp, sc in sp between roll st and next dc, sc in next 8 sts, sc in sp between dc and next roll st, *hdc in next sp between roll sts, 2 dc in next sp, ch 2, 2 dc in next sp, hdc in next sp, sc in sp between roll st and next dc, sc in next 8 sts, sc in sp between dc and next roll st, rep from * twice more, join in 2nd ch of beg ch-2. Fasten off.
**Rnd 8:** Attach A with sc in any ch-2 sp, 3 sc in same sp, sc in next 16 sts, *4 sc in next ch-2 sp, sc in next 16 sts, rep from * twice more; join in first sc. Fasten off.

## SECOND MOTIF
Work same as Rnds 1–8 of First Motif.
**Rnd 9 (joining rnd):** Attach A with sc in 3rd sc of any 4-sc group, ch 2, sl st in corresponding sc on adjacent motif, *ch 2, on working motif, sk next sc, sl st in next sc, ch 2, on adjacent motif, sk next sc, sl st in next sc; rep from * 8 times more. Fasten off.

## REMAINING MOTIFS

Referring to Assembly Diagram for placement, work as for Second Motif, joining to adjacent motifs in similar manner and making sure all 4-corner joinings are secure.

## BORDER

***Note:*** *For **sc dec**, draw up lp in each of 2 sts indicated, yo and draw through all 3 lps on hook.*

**Rnd 1:** Attach A with sc in 3rd sc of 4-sc group as indicated on Assembly Diagram, 2 sc in same sp, sc in each st and ch-2 joining around, working 3 sc in each outer corner, join with sl st in first sc.

**Rnd 2:** Ch 1, sc in same sc, 3 sc in next sc, sc in each sc around working 3 sc in 2nd sc of each 3-sc group and working **sc dec** *(see Note)* over 2 sc at each inner corner, join in first sc.

Fasten off and weave in all ends. ❧

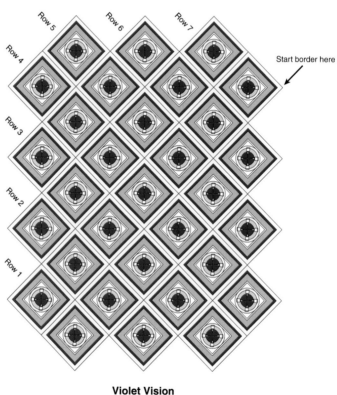

**Violet Vision**
Assembly Diagram

# WEDDING WREATHS

Design by Tammy Hildebrand

## FINISHED SIZE

Approximately 40 x 62 inches

## MATERIALS

- TLC Lustre medium (worsted) weight (5 oz/253 yds/141g per skein): 6 skeins #5017 natural (A), 2 skeins #5660 light sage (B) and 1 skein #5730 coral rose (C)
- Size J/10/6mm crochet hook or size needed to obtain gauge

## GAUGE

Rnds 1–8 of motif = 9½ inches across

To save time, take time to check gauge.

## SPECIAL STITCHES

For **beginning cluster (beg cl):** Ch 3, keeping last lp of each dc on hook, work 2 dc in same sp or st, yo and draw through all 3 lps on hook.

For **cluster (cl):** Keeping last lp of each dc on hook, work 3 dc in same sp or st, yo and draw through all 4 lps on hook.

For **popcorn (pc):** 3 dc in same sp or st, drop lp from hook, insert hook from front to back through first dc, pick up dropped lp and draw through lp on hook.

For **joining ch-3 sp:** Ch 1, drop lp, insert hook in center ch of corresponding ch-3 sp on previous motif, pick up dropped lp and draw through, ch 1.

## PATTERN NOTE

Join with slip stitch unless otherwise stated.

## FIRST ROW
## FIRST MOTIF

**Rnd 1:** With A ch 3, join to form ring, ch 3 *(counts as dc)*, 15 dc in ring, join in 3rd ch of beg ch-3. *(16 dc)*

**Rnd 2:** Ch 1, sc in same st as joining, ch 3, *sk next st, sc in next st, ch 3; rep from * 6 times more, join in first sc. Fasten off. *(8 ch-3 sps)*

**Rnd 3:** Join B with sl st in any ch-3 sp, [**beg cl** *(see Special Stitches),* ch 2, **cl** *(see Special Stitches)*] in same sp, ch 1, *(cl, ch 2, cl) in next ch-3 sp, ch 1; rep from * 6 times more, join in top of beg cl. Fasten off.

**Rnd 4:** Join C with sc in any ch-1 sp, ch 3, *pc *(see Special Stitches)* in next ch-2 sp, ch 3, sc in next ch-1 sp, ch 3; rep from * 6 times more, pc in next ch-2 sp, ch 3; join in first sc. Fasten off.

**Rnd 5:** Join A with sl st in any sc, ch 3, 4 dc in same st, (sc, ch 3, sc) in next pc, *5 dc in next sc, (sc, ch 3, sc) in top of next pc; rep from * 6 times more, join in 3rd ch of beg ch-3.

**Rnd 6:** Ch 3, sk next dc, (dc, ch 1, dc) in next dc, sk next dc, dc in next st, (2 dc, ch 2, 2 dc) in next ch-3 sp, *sk next sc, dc in next dc, sk next dc, (dc, ch 1, dc) in next dc, sk next dc, dc in next dc, (2 dc, ch 2, 2 dc) in next ch-3 sp; rep from * 6 times more, join in 3rd ch of beg ch-3. Fasten off.

**Rnd 7:** Join B with sc in any ch-2 sp, (ch 1, sc) in same sp, [ch 1, sk next st, sc in next st] twice, ch 1, sk next ch-1 sp, [sc in next st, ch 1, sk next st] twice, *(sc, ch 1, sc) in next ch-2 sp, [ch 1, sk next st, sc in next st] twice, ch 1, sk next ch-1 sp; rep from * 6 times more, [sc in next st, ch 1, sk next st] twice, join in first sc. Fasten off.

**Rnd 8:** Join A with sl st in any ch-1 sp, ch 6 *(counts as a dc and ch-3 sp),* (dc, ch 3, dc, ch 3, dc) in same sp, sk next ch-1 sp and next sc, working over ch-1 sps of Rnd 7 in skipped sts of Rnd 6, sc in next skipped dc, (dc, ch 3, dc) in next skipped ch-1 sp, sc in next skipped dc, *sk next sc and ch-1 sp, (dc, ch 3) 3 times in next ch-1 sp, dc in same sp, sk next

ch-1 sp and next sc, working over ch-1 sps of Rnd 7 in skipped sts of Rnd 6, sc in next skipped dc, (dc, ch 3, dc) in next skipped ch-1 sp, sc in next skipped dc; rep from * 6 times more, join in 3rd ch of beg ch-6. Fasten off.

## SECOND MOTIF

Work same as Rnds 1–7 of First Motif.

**Rnd 8 (joining rnd):** Join A with sl st in any ch-1 sp, ch 6 (counts as dc and ch 3), [dc, **joining ch-3 sp** (see Special Stitches), dc, joining ch-3 sp, dc] in same sp, sk next ch-1 sp and next sc, working over ch-1 sps of Rnd 7 in skipped sts of Rnd 6, sc in next skipped dc, (dc, joining ch-3 sp, dc) in next skipped ch-1 sp, sc in next skipped dc, sk next sc and ch-1 sp, (dc, joining ch-3 sp) twice in next ch-1 sp, (dc, ch 3, dc) in same sp, sk next ch-1 sp and next sc, working over ch-1 sps of Rnd 7 in skipped sts of Rnd 6, sc in next skipped dc, (dc, ch 3, dc) in next skipped ch-1 sp, sc in next skipped dc, *sk next sc and ch-1 sp, (dc, ch 3) 3 times in next ch-1 sp, dc in same sp, sk next ch-1 sp and next sc, working over ch-1 sps of Rnd 7 in skipped sts of Rnd 6, sc in next skipped dc, (dc, ch 3, dc) in next skipped ch-1 sp, sc in next skipped dc, rep from * 5 times more, join in 3rd ch of beg ch-6. Fasten off.

Rep Second Motif twice more for a total of 4 motifs in this row.

## SECOND ROW
### FIRST MOTIF

Work same as Second Motif on First Row joining to First Motif on First Row in similar manner.

## SECOND MOTIF

Work same as Rnds 1–7 of First Motif on First Row.

**Rnd 8 (joining rnd):** Join A with sl st in any ch-1 sp, ch 6 (counts as dc and ch-3), joining to side of last Motif, work (dc, joining ch-3 sp, dc, joining ch sp, dc) in same sp, sk next ch-1 sp and next sc, working over ch-1 sps of Rnd 7 in sk sts of Rnd 6, sc in next sk dc, (dc, joining ch-3 sp, dc) in next sk ch-1 sp, sc in next sk dc, sk next sc and ch-1 sp, (dc, joining ch-

3 sp) twice in next ch-1 sp, (dc, ch 3, dc) in same sp, sk next ch-1 sp and next sc, working over ch-1 sps of rnd 7 in skipped sts of rnd 6, sc in next skipped dc, (dc, ch 3, dc) in next skipped ch-1 sp, sc in next skipped dc, sk next sc and next ch-1 sp, (dc, ch 3, dc) in next ch-1 sp, (joining ch-3 sp, dc) in same sp, sk next ch-1 sp and next sc, working over ch-1 sps of rnd 7 in skipped sts of rnd 6, sc in next skipped dc, (dc, joining ch-3 sp, dc) in next skipped ch-1 sp, sc in next skipped dc, sk next sc and ch-1 sp, (dc, joining ch-3 sp) twice in next ch-1 sp, (dc, ch 3, dc) in same sp, sk next ch-1 sp and next sc, working over ch-1 sps of rnd 7 in skipped sts of rnd 6, sc in next skipped dc, (dc, ch 3, dc) in next skipped ch-1 sp, sc in next skipped dc, *sk next sc and ch-1 sp, (dc, ch 3) 3 times in next ch-1 sp, dc in same sp, sk next ch-1 sp and next sc, sk next ch-1 sp and next sc, working over ch-1 sps of rnd 7 in skipped sts of rnd 6, sc in next skipped dc, (dc, ch 3, dc) in next skipped ch-1 sp, sc in next skipped dc; rep from * 3 times more, join in 3rd ch of beg ch-6. Fasten off.

Rep Second Motif twice more for a total of 4 motifs in this row.

## REMAINING ROWS

Work same Second Row.

## FILLER MOTIF

**Rnd 1:** With C, ch 3, join to form a ring, ch 3, 2 dc in ring, ch 2, (3 dc in ring, ch 2) 3 times, join in 3rd ch of beg ch-3. Fasten off.

**Rnd 2:** Join B with an sc in any ch-2 sp, 2 sc in same sp, sk next st, 3 sc in next st, *3 sc in next ch-2 sp, sk next st, 3 sc in next st, rep from * twice more, join in first sc. Fasten off.

**Rnd 3 (joining rnd):** Join A in center sc of any 3-sc group, ch 3, joining ch-3 sp in center ch-3 sp of open sps between motifs, dc in same sc on filler, *working joining ch-3 sp in next ch-3 sp, motif joining and next ch-3 sp on next motif, (dc, joining ch-3 sp) 3 times in center sc of next 3-sc group, dc in same sc, (dc, joining ch-3 sp, dc) in center sc of next 3-sc group, rep from * twice more, working joining ch sp in next ch-3 sp, motif joining and next ch-3 sp on next motif, (dc, joining ch-3 sp) 3 times in center st of next 3-sc group, dc in same st, join in 3rd ch of beg ch-3. Fasten off.

## BORDER

Holding afghan with RS facing and one short end at top and working around outer edge, join A with a sc in center ch-3 sp in upper right-hand corner, 5 dc in next ch-3 sp, 3 tr in next ch-3 sp, 5 dc in next ch-3 sp, sc in next ch-3 sp, 5 dc in next ch-3 sp, 3 tr in next ch-3 sp, 5 dc in next ch-3 sp, *[tr in center of motif joining, {5 dc in next ch-3 sp, 3 tr in next ch-3 sp, 5 dc in next ch-3 sp, sc in next ch-3 sp} twice, 5 dc in next ch-3 sp, 3 tr in next ch-3 sp, 5 dc in next ch-3 sp] twice, tr in center of motif joining, {5 dc in next ch-3 sp, 3 tr in next ch-3 sp, 5 dc in next ch-3 sp, sc in next ch-3 sp} 4 times, 5 dc in next ch-3 sp, 3 tr in next ch-3 sp, 5 dc in next ch-3 sp, [tr in center of motif joining, {5 dc in next ch-3 sp, 3 tr in next ch-3 sp, 5 dc in next ch-3 sp, sc in next ch-3 sp} twice, 5 dc in next ch-3 sp, 3 tr in next ch-3 sp, 5 dc in next ch-3 sp] 4 times, tr in center of motif joining, {5 dc in next ch-3 sp, 3 tr in next ch-3 sp, 5 dc in next ch-3 sp, sc in next ch-3 sp} 4 times, 5 dc in next ch-3 sp, 3 tr in next ch-3 sp, 5 dc in next ch-3 sp **, rep from * ending at **, tr in center of motif joining, {5 dc in next ch-3 sp, 3 tr in next ch-3 sp, 5 dc in next ch-3 sp, sc in next ch-3 sp} twice, 5 dc in next ch-3 sp, 3 tr in next ch-3 sp, 5 dc in next ch-3 sp join in first sc. Fasten off and weave in all ends. ❧

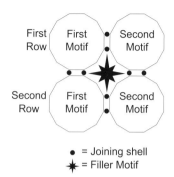

● = Joining shell
✸ = Filler Motif

**Wedding Wreath**
Assembly Diagram

# DREAM GARDEN

Design by Diane Poellot

## FINISHED SIZE
Approximately 56 x 79 inches

## MATERIALS
- Red Heart Super Saver medium (worsted) weight yarn (8 oz/452 yds/225g per skein): 1 skein each #531 light plum (C), #380 Windsor blue (E), #320 cornmeal (G), #374 country rose (H) and #362 spruce (I), #373 petal pink (J), #774 light raspberry (M) and #358 lavender (N)
- Red Heart Classic medium (worsted) weight yarn (3½ oz/198 yds/99g per skein): 7 skeins #760 new berry (A), 3 skeins #252 medium coral (B), 1 skein each #882 country blue (D), #683 light seafoam (F), #827 light periwinkle (K), #684 seafoam (L), #645 honey gold (O) and #755 pale rose (P)
- Size J/10/6mm crochet hook or size needed to obtain gauge

## GAUGE
Rnds 1–3 of motif = 5 inches from corner to corner
To save time, take time to check gauge.

## PATTERN NOTE
Join with slip stitch unless otherwise stated.

## FIRST MOTIF
**Rnd 1:** With B, ch 4, join with sl st to form ring, ch 6, (2 dc in ring, ch 3) 5 times, dc in ring, join in 3rd ch of beg ch-6.

**Dream Garden**

**Rnd 2:** Sl st in next ch-3 sp, ch 3 *(counts as dc),* 4 dc in same sp, [5 dc in next ch-3 sp] 5 times, join in 3rd ch of beg ch-3.

**Rnd 3:** Sl st in next dc, ch 3, 5 dc in next dc, dc in next dc, *sk next 2 dc, dc in next dc, 5 dc in next dc, dc in next dc, rep from * 5 times more, join in 3rd ch of beg ch-3. Fasten off.

**Rnd 4:** Attach A with sc in dc before any 5-dc group, sc in next dc, *(2 sc in next dc) 3 times, sc in next 2 dc, ch 5, sl st by inserting hook under 2 center

**Dream Garden**
Assembly Diagram

strands at base of dc (between petals) on Rnd 1, ch 5, sc in next 2 dc on working rnd; rep from * around, join with sl st in first sc. Fasten off.

## SECOND MOTIF

Referring to Assembly Diagram for color and placement, work same as Rnds 1–3 of First Motif .

**Rnd 4 (joining rnd):** Attach B with sc in dc before any 5-dc group, sc in next dc, [2 sc in next dc, sc in next dc, sl st between corresponding dc on adjacent motif, sc in same st as last sc, 2 sc in next dc, sc in next 2 dc, ch 5, sl st by inserting hook under 2 center strands at base of dc (between petals) on Rnd 1, ch 5, sc in next 2 dc] around, joining where needed. Fasten off.

## REMAINING MOTIFS

Referring to Assembly Diagram for motif color and placement, work rem motifs as for Second Motif and joining in similar manner to all adjacent motifs. ❧

# PURE PLEASURE Continued from page 31

**Rnd 4:** Attach C in any ch-1 sp, **beg tr cl** (see Special Stitches) in same sp, ch 2, [**tr cl** (see Special Stitches) in next ch-1 sp, ch 2] 19 times, join in top of beg tr cl. Fasten off. (20 tr cls and 20 ch-2 sps)

**Rnd 5:** Attach B in any ch-2 sp, ch 4 (counts as tr), (2 tr, ch 2, 3 tr) in same place (beg corner), *(2 dc, hdc) in next ch-2 sp, 4 sc in each of next 2 ch-2 sps, (hdc, 2 dc) in next ch-2 sp**, (3 tr, ch 2, 3 tr) in next ch-2 sp (corner); rep from * 3 times more, ending last rep at **, join in 4th ch of beg ch-4.

**Rnd 6:** Sl st in each of next 2 tr, sl st in corner ch-2 sp, ch 3, (dc, ch 2, 2 dc) in same sp, *[ch 1, sk next st, dc in next st] 10 times, ch 1**, (2 dc, ch 2, 2 dc) in next corner ch-2 sp, rep from * 3 times more, ending last rep at **, join in 3rd ch of beg ch-3. Fasten off.

**Rnd 7:** Attach A in the first ch-1 sp to left of any corner group, ch 1, sc in same sp, *[**puff st** (see Special Stitches) around next dc, sc in next ch-1 sp] 10 times, puff st around each of next 2 dc of corner group, (2 sc, ch 1, 2 sc) in corner ch-2 sp, puff st around each of next 2 dc of corner group **, sc in next ch-1 sp, rep from * 3 times more, ending last rep at **, join in first sc. Fasten off.

**Rnd 8:** Attach B in any corner ch-1 sp, ch 3, (2 dc, ch 3, 3 dc) in same sp (beg corner shell), *sk next 4 sts, [(2 dc, ch 1, 2 dc) in next st (shell), sk next 4 sts] 5 times**, (3 dc, ch 3, 3 dc) in next corner ch-1 sp (corner shell), rep from * 3 times, ending last rep at **, join in 3rd ch of beg ch-3. Fasten off.

## SECOND MOTIF

Work same as Rnds 1–7 of First Motif.

**Rnd 8 (joining rnd):** Attach B in any corner ch-1 sp, ch 3, (2 dc, ch 3, 3 dc) in same sp (beg corner shell), sk next 4 sts, [(2 dc, ch 1, 2 dc) in next st (shell), sk next 4 sts] 5 times, 3 dc in next ch-1 sp, ch 1, sl st in corresponding corner shell ch-1 sp on adjacent motif, ch 1, 3 dc in same sp on working motif, sk next 4 sts, [2 dc in st, sl st in ch-1 sp of next shell on adjacent motif, 2 dc in same st on working motif; sk next 4 sts] 5 times; 3 dc in next ch-1 sp, ch 1, sl st in next corner ch-1 sp on adjacent motif, ch 1, 3 dc in same ch-1 sp on working motif, sk next 4 sts, [(2 dc, ch 1, 2 dc) in next st (shell), sk next 4 sts] 5 times; (3 dc, ch 3, 3 dc) in next corner ch-1 sp (corner shell); [(2 dc, ch 1, 2 dc) in next st (shell), sk next 4 sts] 5 times; join in 3rd ch of beg ch-3. Fasten off.

## REMAINING MOTIFS

Referring to Assembly Diagram for motif placement, work rem motifs as for Second Motif joining to adjacent motifs in similar manner making sure all 4-corner joinings are secure. ❧

# COOL SQUARES

The only thing these afghans have in common is that they are all made up of squares and rectangles. You'll love their innovative qualities!

# SOPHISTICATED ZIGZAG

Design by Joyce Nordstrom

## FINISHED SIZE
Approximately 48 x 70 inches

## MATERIALS
- TLC Essentials (6 oz/326 yds/170g per skein): 4 skeins #2313 aran (A)
- TLC Heathers (5 oz/277 yds/141g per skein): 4 skeins #2452 mulberry heather (B) and 3 skeins #2451 light mulberry heather (C)
- Size I/9/5.5mm crochet hook or size needed to obtain gauge

## GAUGE
Rnds 1–3 of motif = 4 inches square

## SPECIAL STITCHES
For **popcorn (pc):** 4 dc in st indicated, drop last lp from hook, insert hook in first dc and draw dropped lp through, ch 1.

For **beginning petal (beg petal):** Ch 3, [yo, draw up lp in same st, yo and draw through 2 lps on hook] twice, yo and draw through all 3 lps on hook.

For **petal (petal):** Yo, draw up lp in st just worked, yo and draw through 2 lps on hook, [yo, draw up lp in next st, yo and draw through 2 lps on hook] twice, yo and draw through all 4 lps on hook.

## PATTERN NOTE
Join with slip stitch unless otherwise stated.

## FIRST ROW
## FIRST MOTIF
## POPCORN MOTIF

**Rnd 1:** With B ch 4, join to form a ring, ch 3 *(counts as dc)*, 15 dc in ring, join in 3rd ch of beg ch-3. *(16 dc)*

**Rnd 2:** Ch 3, *dc in next st, **pc** *(see Special Stitches)*

in next dc, dc in next 2 dc**; ch 4 *(corner),* dc in next dc; rep from * 3 times more, ending last rep at **, ch 2, hdc in 3rd ch of beg ch-3.

**Rnd 3:** Ch 1, [sc in sp formed by hdc, ch 1] twice, *sk next dc, sc in next dc, ch 1, sk next pc, sc in next dc, ch 1, sk next dc, (sc, ch 1, sc, ch 3, sc, ch 1, sc, ch 1) in next corner ch-4 sp; rep from * twice more, sk next dc, sc in next dc, ch 1, sk next pc, sc in next dc, ch 1, sk next dc, (sc, ch 1, sc, ch 3) in beg corner sp, join in first sc. Fasten off.

## SECOND ROW
## FIRST MOTIF
## POPCORN MOTIF
Work same as First Motif in First Row.

## SECOND MOTIF
## POPCORN MOTIF
Work same as Rnds 1 and 2 of First Motif of First Row.

**Rnd 3 (joining rnd):** Ch 1, [sc in sp formed by joining hdc, ch 1] twice; sk next dc, sc in next dc, ch 1, sk next pc, sc in next dc, ch 1, sk next dc, (sc, ch 1) twice in corner ch-4 sp, sl st in corresponding corner ch-4 sp of adjacent motif, *ch 1, (sc, ch 1) twice in same sp on working motif, sc in next dc, ch 1, sl st in next ch-1 sp of adjacent motif, ch 1, sc in next dc, ch 1, (sc, ch 1) twice in next corner ch-4 sp, sl st in corresponding corner sp of adjacent motif, rep from * once more, ch 1, (sc, ch 1) twice in same sp on working motif, sk next dc, sc in next dc, ch 1, sk next pc, sc in next dc, ch 1, sk next dc, (sc, ch 1, sc, ch 3) in beg corner sp, join in first sc.

## THIRD MOTIF
## PETAL MOTIF

**Rnd 1:** With A, ch 4, to form a ring, ch 3 *(counts as dc),*

15 dc in ring; join with sl st in 3rd ch of beg ch-3. *(16 dc)*

**Rnd 2: Beg petal** *(see Special Stitches),* *ch 3, **petal** *(see Special Stitches)* **, ch 4 *(corner),* petal; rep from * 3 times more, ending last rep at **, ch 2, hdc in top of beg petal.

**Rnd 3 (joining to petal rnd):** Ch 1, [sc in sp formed by joining hdc, ch 1] twice; sk next petal, (sc, ch 1) twice in next ch-3 sp; sk next petal, (sc, ch 1, sc, ch 3, sc, ch 1, sc, ch 1) in corner ch-4 sp, sk next petal, (sc, ch 1) twice in next ch-3 sp, sk next petal, (sc, ch 1) twice in next corner ch-4 sp, sl st in corresponding ch-4 sp on adjacent motif, ch 1, (sc, ch 1) twice in same sp on working motif, sk next petal, sc in next ch-3 sp, ch 1, sl st in corresponding ch-1 sp on adjacent motif, sc in same ch-3 sp on working motif, ch 1, sk next petal, (sc, ch 1, sc, ch 3, sc, ch 1, sc, ch 1) in corner ch-4 sp, sk next petal, (sc, ch 1) twice in next ch-3 sp, sk next petal, (sc, ch 1, sc, ch 3) in beg corner; join in first sc. Fasten off.

**Rnd 3 (joining to pc rnd):** Ch 1, [sc in sp formed by joining hdc, ch 1] twice, *sk next dc, sc in next dc, ch 1, sk next pc, sc in next dc, ch 1, sk next dc, (sc, ch 1) twice in corner ch-4 sp, sl st in corresponding corner ch-4 sp of adjacent motif, ch 1, (sc, ch 1) twice in same corner sp on working motif, sk next dc, sc in next dc, ch 1, sl st in corresponding ch-1 sp on adjacent motif, ch 1, sc in next dc on working motif, ch 1, sk next dc, (sc, ch 1) twice in next corner ch-4 sp, sl st in corresponding ch-4 corner sp on adjacent motif, (sc, ch 1) twice in same corner on working motif, ch 1, sk next dc, sc in next dc, ch 1, sk next pc, sc in next dc, ch 1, sk next dc, (sc, ch 1, sc, ch 3, sc, ch 1, sc, ) in next corner ch-4 sp, ch 1, sk next dc, sc in next dc, ch 1, sk next pc, sc in next dc, ch 1, (sc, ch 1, sc, ch 3) in beg corner, join in first sc.

## REMAINING MOTIFS

*Note:* On Assembly Diagram Color A motifs are petal motifs, and Color B and C motifs are popcorn motifs. Referring to Assembly Diagram for color, type (petal or popcorn) and placement, work rem motifs in similar manner joining to adjacent motifs.

## BORDER

*Note:* For **dec,** [yo, draw up lp in next ch-3 sp]

twice, yo and draw through all 5 lps on hook.

**Rnd 1:** Attach C in corner sp indicated; ch 3 *(counts as hdc, ch 1),* *[hdc in next ch-1 sp, ch 1] 5 times; **dec** *(see Note)* [hdc in next ch-1 sp, ch 1] 5 times, [hdc, ch 3, hdc] in next ch-3 corner sp, rep from * around, making any necessary adjustments for outside or inside corner sps, ending with hdc in beg corner, ch 3, sl st in 2nd ch of beg ch 3. Fasten off.

**Rnd 2:** With A, rep Rnd 1.

**Rnd 3:** With B, rep Rnd 1, ending last rep with hdc in beg corner, ch 1, hdc in 2nd ch of beg ch-3. **Do not fasten off.**

**Rnd 4:** Working from **left to right**, sc in sp formed by joining hdc, ch 1; [sc in next ch-1 sp, ch 1] 15 times; (sc, ch 2, sc, ch 1) in next outside corner, [sc in next ch-1 sp, ch 1] 5 times, sk next hdc, sc in next ch-1 sp, sc in next hdc, sc in next ch-1 sp, ch 1 for inside corner; continue around adjusting as necessary for inside and outside corners, ending with sc in beg corner, ch 2, sl st in first sc.

Fasten off and weave in all ends. 🐦

**Sophisticated Zigzag**
Assembly Diagram

# BLAZING EMBERS

Design by Ann E. Smith

## FINISHED SIZE

Approximately 48 x 56 inches

## MATERIALS

- Red Heart Classic medium (worsted) weight yarn (3.5 oz/198 yds/100g per skein): 2 skeins each #252 medium coral (A), #760 new berry (B), #914 country red (C), #762 claret (D), #286 bronze (E), #761 light berry (F) and #289 copper (G); 1 skein each #755 pale rose (H), #759 cameo rose (I), #719 lily pink (J) and #0246 sea coral (K)
- Size H/8/5mm crochet hook or size needed to obtain gauge

## GAUGE

Rnds 1–10 of motif = 7 inches square
To save time, take time to check gauge.

## SPECIAL STITCH

For **front post double crochet (fpdc):** Yo, insert hook from front to back around **post** (see Stitch Guide) of st indicated, yo and pull up a lp, (yo, and draw through 2 lps on hook) twice.

## PATTERN NOTES

Afghan is made with 5 different motif color combinations. Refer to Assembly Diagram for placement of motifs.
Join with slip stitch unless otherwise stated.

## FIRST ROW
## MOTIF A

**Rnd 1 (RS):** With A, ch 4; 15 dc in 4th ch (beg 3 sk chs count as a dc) from hook; join in 3rd ch of beg 3 skipped chs. Fasten off. (16 sts)

**Rnd 2:** Attach B with sc in any dc, [**fpdc** (see Special Stitch) around next dc, sc in next dc] 7 times, fpdc around last dc, join in first sc. Fasten off.

**Rnd 3:** Attach C with sc in any sc, sc in same sc, [fpdc around next fpdc, 2 sc in next sc] 7 times, fpdc around next fpdc, join in first sc. Fasten off. (24 sts)

**Rnd 4:** Attach D with sc in first sc of any 2-sc group, sc in same sc, 2 sc in next sc, [fpdc around next fpdc, 2 sc in each of next 2 sc] 7 times, fpdc around next fpdc, join in first sc. Fasten off. (40 sts)

**Rnd 5:** Attach H with sc in sc to left of any fpdc, sc in same sc, sc in next 2 sc, 2 sc in next sc, [fpdc around next fpdc, 2 sc in next sc, sc in next 2 sc, 2 sc in next sc] 7 times, fpdc around next fpdc; join in first sc. Fasten off. (56 sts)

**Rnd 6:** Attach I with sc in any sc to left of fpdc, sc in next 5 sc, [3 fpdc around next fpdc (corner made), sc in next 6 sc, fpdc around next fpdc, sc in next 6 sc] 3 times, 3 fpdc around next fpdc (corner made), sc in next 6 sc, fpdc around next fpdc, join in first sc. Fasten off. (64 sts)

**Rnd 7:** Attach D with sc in sc to left of any single fpdc, sc in next 5 sc, *fpdc around next fpdc, 3 fpdc around next fpdc, fpdc around next fpdc, sc in next 6 sc, fpdc around next fpdc **, sc in next 6 sc; rep from * around, ending last rep at **; join in first sc. Fasten off. (72 sts)

**Rnd 8:** Attach C with sc in sc to left of any single fpdc, sc next 5 sc, *fpdc around each of next 2 fpdc, 3 fpdc around next fpdc, fpdc around each of next 2 fpdc, sc in next 6 sc, fpdc around next fpdc **, sc in next 6 sc; rep from * around, ending last rep at **; join in first sc. **Do not fasten off.** (80 sts)

**Rnd 9:** Ch 1, sc in same sc and in each of next 5 sc, sc in next 3 fpdc, *3 sc in next fpdc, sc in next 3 fpdc, sc in next 6 sc and in next fpdc **, sc in 6 sc

and in next 3 fpdc; rep from * around, ending last rep at **; join in first sc. Fasten off. *(88 sts)*

**Rnd 10:** Attach E with sc in any corner sc, (ch 2, sc) in same sc, *[ch 1, sk next sc, sc in next sc] 10 times, ch 1, sk next sc **, (sc, ch 2, sc) in next sc; rep from * around, ending last rep at **; join in first sc. Fasten off.

**Rnd 11 (joining rnd):** Working around Motif A, attach G with sc in corner ch-2 sp, (ch 2, sc) in same sp,*[ch 1, sc in next ch-1 sp] 11 times **, (ch 1, sc, ch 2, sc) in corner ch-2 sp; rep from * around, ending last rep at **; join in first sc. Fasten off. *(Motif completed.)*

## MOTIF B

Work same as Rnds 1–10 of Motif A in following color sequence:

**Rnds 1–4:** With K.
**Rnd 5:** With F.
**Rnd 6:** With C.
**Rnd 7:** With D.
**Rnd 8:** With H.
**Rnd 9:** With I.
**Rnd 10:** With E.

**Rnd 11 (1-side joining):** Attach G with sc in corner ch-2 sp, (ch 2, sc) in same sp, [ch 1, sc in next ch-1 sp] 11 times, ch 1, sc in corner ch-2 sp, ch 1, drop lp from hook, insert hook from RS to WS through corresponding ch-2 sp on adjacent motif, pull dropped lp through, ch 1, sc in same sp on working motif, *ch 1, drop lp from hook, insert hook from RS to WS through corresponding ch-1 sp on adjacent motif, pull dropped lp through, ch 1, sc in next ch-1 sp on working motif, rep from * 10 times more, ch 1, sc in corner ch-2 sp, ch 1, drop lp from hook, insert hook from RS to WS through corresponding ch-2 sp on adjacent motif, pull dropped lp through, ch 1, sc in same sp on working motif, [ch 1, sc in next ch-1 sp] 11 times, ch 1, (sc, ch 2, sc) in next corner ch-2 sp, [ch 1, sc in next ch-1 sp] 11 times, ch 1, join with sl st in first sc. Fasten off. *(Motif completed.)*

## MOTIF C

Work same as Rnds 1–10 of Motif A in following color sequence:

**Rnds 1–3:** With I.
**Rnd 4:** With J.
**Rnds 5 & 6:** With D.
**Rnd 7:** With K.
**Rnd 8:** With A.
**Rnd 9:** With F.
**Rnd 10:** With E.
**Rnd 11:** Work same as Rnd 11 of Motif B.

## MOTIF D

Work same as Rnds 1–10 of Motif A in following color sequence:

**Rnd 1:** With D.
**Rnds 2 & 3:** With K.
**Rnd 4:** With C.
**Rnds 5 & 6:** With F.
**Rnd 7:** With A.
**Rnds 8 & 9:** With B.
**Rnd 10:** With E.
**Rnd 11:** Work same as Rnd 11 of Motif B.

## MOTIF E

Work same as Rnds 1–10 of Motif A in following color sequence:

**Rnd 1:** With J.
**Rnd 2:** With I.
**Rnd 3:** With H.
**Rnd 4:** With B.
**Rnd 5:** With F.
**Rnd 6:** With A.
**Rnd 7:** With D.
**Rnds 8 & 9:** With A.
**Rnd 10:** With E.
**Rnd 11:** Work same as Rnd 11 of Motif B. For last motif in First Row work same as Rnds 1–10 of Motif A. Work Rnd 11 same as Rnd 11 of Motif B.

## SECOND ROW
### FIRST MOTIF
Referring to Assembly Diagram for motif, work Rnds 1–10, join as for Rnd 11 of Motif B (1-side joining).

### SECOND MOTIF
Referring to Assembly Diagram for motif, work Rnds 1–10.

**Rnd 11 (2-side joining):** Attach G with sc in corner ch-2 sp, (ch 2, sc) in same sp, [ch 1, sc in next ch-1 sp] 11 times, ch 1, sc in corner ch-2 sp, ch 1, drop lp from hook, insert hook from RS to WS through corresponding ch-2 sp on adjacent motif, pull dropped lp through, ch 1, sc in same sp on working motif, [*ch 1, drop lp from hook, insert hook from RS to WS through corresponding ch-1 sp on adjacent motif, pull dropped lp through, ch 1, sc in next ch-1 sp on working motif, rep from * 10 times more, ch 1, sc in corner ch-2 sp, ch 1, drop lp from hook, insert hook from RS to WS through corresponding corner joining on adjacent motifs, pull dropped lp through, ch 1, sc in same sp on working motif], rep between [ ] once, [ch 1, sc in next ch-1 sp] 11 times, ch 1, join with sl st in first sc. Fasten off. *(Motif completed.)*

Refer to Assembly Diagram for remaining motif placement, joining as for previous motifs in Rnd 11.

## BORDER
**Rnd 1:** Attach F with sc in any corner ch-2 sp, (ch 2, sc) in same sp, *(ch 1, sc in next ch-1 sp) to next corner ch-2 sp, ch 1, (sc, ch 2, sc) in corner ch-2 sp, rep from * twice more, (ch 1, sc in next ch-1 sp) to beg corner, ch 1, join with sl st in first sc. Fasten off.
**Rnd 2:** With E, rep Rnd 1.
**Rnd 3:** With G, rep Rnd 1.
**Rnd 4:** With B, rep Rnd 1.
**Rnd 5:** With E, rep Rnd 1.
**Rnd 6:** With C, rep Rnd 1. At end of rnd **do not fasten off.**
**Rnd 7:** Sl st in next corner ch-1 sp, ch 1, 3 sc in

same sp; *2 sc in each ch-1 sp to next corner ch-2 sp, 3 sc in next corner ch-2 sp; rep from * twice more, 2 sc in each ch-1 sp to beg corner, join with sl st in first sc.
Fasten off and weave in all ends. ❧

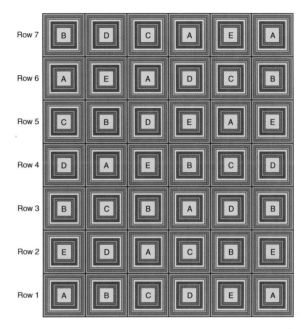

**Blazing Embers**
Assembly Diagram

# BRILLIANT BUTTERFLY

Design by Martha Brooks Stein

## FINISHED SIZE
Approximately 44 x 58 inches

## MATERIALS
- Red Heart Kids medium (worsted) weight yarn (5 oz/302 yds/140g per skein): 5 skeins #2001 white (A), 2 skeins each #2252 orange (B), #2230 yellow (C), #2652 lime (D), #2347 periwinkle (D); 1 skein each #2734 pink (F) and #2360 orchid (G)
- TLC Essentials medium (worsted) weight yarn (6 oz/326 yds/170g per skein): 1 skein #2112 black (H)
- Size I/9/5.5mm crochet hook or size needed to obtain gauge

## GAUGE
Motif = 2½ inches square

## PATTERN NOTE
Join with slip stitch unless otherwise stated.

## FIRST ROW
### FIRST MOTIF
**Rnd 1:** With A ch 4, join to form ring, ch 2 *(counts as a dc)*, 2 dc in ring, (ch 2, 3 dc in ring) 3 times, join with hdc in 2nd ch of beg ch-2.

**Rnd 2:** Ch 2, 2 dc in sp formed by joining hdc, ch 1, [(3 dc, ch 2, 3 dc) in next ch-2 corner sp, ch 1] 3 times, 3 dc in beg corner, ch 2, join in 2nd ch of beg ch-2. Fasten off.

### SECOND MOTIF
**Rnd 1:** Referring to Assembly Diagram for color and placement, work same as Rnd 1 of First Motif.

**Rnd 2 (1-side joining):** Ch 2, 2 dc in sp formed by joining hdc, ch 1, (3 dc, ch 2, 3 dc) in next corner sp, ch 1, 3 dc in next corner sp, ch 1, holding WS of completed motif facing WS of working motif, sc in corresponding corner of adjacent motif, 3 dc in same corner sp on working motif, sc in next ch-1 sp of adjacent motif, 3 dc in next corner ch-2 sp on working motif, sc in corresponding corner ch-2 sp on adjacent motif, ch 1, 3 dc in same corner on working motif, ch 1, 3 dc in beg corner, ch 2, join in 2nd ch of beg ch-2. Fasten off.

## REMAINING MOTIFS
Referring to Assembly Diagram for color and placement, join rem motifs in same manner as for Second Motif.

## SECOND ROW
### FIRST MOTIF
Referring to Assembly Diagram for color, work same as Second Motif in Row 1.

### SECOND MOTIF
***Note:*** *Refer to Assembly Diagram for color.*
**Rnd 1:** Work same as Rnd 1 of First Motif on Row 1.

**Rnd 2 (2-side joining):** Ch 2, 2 dc in sp formed by joining hdc, ch 1, 3 dc in next corner sp, ch 1, holding WS of previous motif facing WS of working motif, sc in corresponding corner of adjacent motif, 3 dc in same corner sp on working motif, sc in next ch-1 sp of adjacent motif, 3 dc in next corner ch-2 sp on working motif, sc in corresponding corner ch-2 sp on

adjacent motif, 3 dc in same corner on working motif, sc in next ch-1 sp of adjacent motif, 3 dc in next corner ch-2 sp on working motif, sc in corresponding corner ch-2 sp on adjacent motif, 3 dc in same corner on working motif, ch 1, 3 dc in beg corner, ch 2, join in 2nd ch of beg ch-2. Fasten off.

## REMAINING MOTIFS

Referring to Assembly Diagram for motif color work as for motifs in Row 2 joining to adjacent motifs in Rnd 2 and making sure all joinings are secure.

## BORDER

**Rnd 1:** Hold with RS facing and 1 short edge at top, attach A with sl st in **back lp** (see Stitch Guide) of 2nd ch of ch-2 sp in upper right-hand corner, ch 1, sc in same sp, *working in back lps only sc in each dc, and in each ch to next corner, sc in next ch **, ch 2, sc in next ch; rep * around ending at **, join with dc in first sc.

**Rnd 2:** Ch 1, sc in sp formed by joining dc, ch 1, sk next sc, *(sc in next sc, ch 1, sk next sc) ** to corner ch-2 sp, (sc, ch 2, sc) in corner sp, ch 1, sk next sc; rep from * around, ending at **, sc in beg corner, join with dc in first sc.

**Rnd 3:** Ch 1, sc in sp formed by joining dc, ch 1, *(sc in next ch-1 sp, ch 1 ) to corner, (sc, ch 2, dc) in corner, ch 1; rep from * around; ending with sc in beg corner sp, join with hdc in first sc.

**Rnd 4:** Ch 6 (counts as dc and ch-3 sp), dc in joining hdc, * (dc, ch 2, dc) in each ch-1 sp to next corner, (dc, ch 3, dc, ch 3, dc) in corner; rep from * around ending with dc in first corner sp, join with dc in 3rd ch of beg ch-6.

**Rnd 5:** Sl st in sp formed by joining dc, (ch 6, dc) in

same sp, (dc, ch 3, dc, ch 3, dc) in next ch-3 corner sp, * (dc, ch 3, dc) in each ch-2 sp across to next corner, (dc, ch 3, dc, ch 3, dc) in each of next 2 ch-3 corner sps; rep from * around, ending with dc in beg corner, join with dc in 3rd ch of beg ch-6.

**Rnd 6:** Sl st in joining dc, (ch 7, dc) in same sp, (dc, ch 4, dc) in each ch-sp around, join in 3rd ch of beg ch-7.

Fasten off and weave in all ends.

## BUTTERFLY ANTENNAE

Referring to Assembly Diagram for placement, hold H behind work. With hook pull lp through to RS as indicated. Work ch on RS to correspond to lines on diagram. 🦋

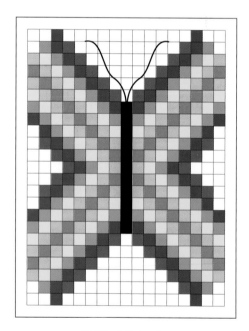

**Brilliant Butterfly**
Assembly Diagram

SKILL LEVEL
■■■□
INTERMEDIATE

YARN WEIGHT
4
MEDIUM

# SPRING PLAID

Design by Joyce Nordstrom

## FINISHED SIZE
Approximately 52 x 68 inches

## MATERIALS
- TLC Essentials (6 oz/326 yds/170g per skein): 3 skeins each #2916 island (A) and #2220 butter (C), 2 skeins each #2316 winter white (B), #2615 light celery (D) and #2880 steel blue (E)
- Size I/9/5.5mm crochet hook or size needed to obtain gauge

## GAUGE
Rnds 1–3 of small square = 3¾ inches square

## SPECIAL STITCHES
For **cluster (cl):** [Yo, pull up lp in sp or st indicated, yo and draw through 2 lps on hook] twice, yo and draw through all 3 lps, ch 1 to close.

For **V-stitch (V-st):** [Dc, ch 1, dc] in st or sp indicated.

For **puff stitch (puff st):** [Yo, pull up lp to height of working row] 4 times in sp or st indicated, yo and draw through all lps on hook, ch 1 to close.

## PATTERN NOTE
Refer to Assembly Diagram for color and placement of motifs, joining to completed motifs in Rnd 2 of motif border.

Join with slip stitch unless otherwise stated.

## SQUARE MOTIF
**Rnd 1:** With A, ch 4; join to form a ring, ch 4 *(counts as dc and ch-1 sp),* [dc in ring, ch 1] 11 times, join in 3rd ch of beg ch-4. *(12 dc)*

**Rnd 2:** Dc in base of ch 3 *(beg cl);* * **cl** *(see Special Stitches)* in next ch-1 sp] twice; [cl **, ch 4, cl] in next

ch-1 sp *(corner);* rep from * 3 times more ending last rep at **; cl in beg sp, ch 2, join with hdc in 3rd ch of beg ch-3.

**Rnd 3:** Ch 1, sc in sp formed by joining hdc;*[ch 1, sc in next sp] 3 times; [sc, ch 3**, sc] in corner sp; rep from * 3 times, ending last rep at **, join in first sc. Fasten off.

## SHORT RECTANGLE MOTIF
**Row 1 (RS):** Referring to Assembly Diagram for color and placement, ch 8; dc in 3rd ch from hook; sk next ch, **V-st** *(see Special Stitches)* in next ch, sk next ch; 2 dc in next ch, turn.

**Row 2:** Ch 3 *(counts as dc),* dc in same ch, ch 1, **puff st** *(see Special Stitches)* in ch-1 sp of next V-st, ch 1, sk next dc, 2 dc 3rd ch of ch-3, turn.

**Row 3:** Ch 3, dc in same sp; V-st in top of puff st; sk dc, 2 dc in 3rd ch of ch-3, turn.

**Rows 4–9:** Rep [Rows 2 and 3] 3 times.

**Row 10:** Rep Row 2. *(5 puff sts in strip)*

## BORDER
**Rnd 1:** Hold with RS facing and Row 10 at top, ch 3, dc in same ch *(beg cl),* working across Row 10, [ch 1, **cl** *(see Special Stitches)* in next ch-1 sp] twice; sk next dc, [cl, ch 4, cl] in next dc, working along side of strip, [ch 1, cl in end of next row] to Row 1; working across end in unused lps of Row 1 [cl, ch 4, cl] in first lp, working across end of strip, [ch 1, cl in sk beg ch] twice, working along other side; [cl, ch 4, cl] in last lp, [ch 1, cl in end of next row] to beg cl, cl in same sp as beg cl, ch 2, join with hdc in top of beg cl. *(10 cls on each side; 4 cls on each end)*

**Rnd 2:** Ch 1, sc in sp formed by joining hdc, *[ch 1, sc in next ch-1 sp] to corner, [sc, ch 4, sc] in corner sp, rep from * around, ending last rep with ch 4; sl st

in first sc. Fasten off. *(11 sc on each side; 5 sc on each end)*

## LONG RECTANGLE MOTIF

**Row 1 (RS):** Referring to Assembly Diagram for color and placement, ch 8; dc in 3rd ch from hook; sk next ch, V-st in next ch, sk next ch; 2 dc in next ch, turn.

**Row 2:** Ch 3 *(counts as dc),* dc in same ch, ch 1, puff st in ch-1 sp of next V-st, ch 1, sk next dc, 2 dc 3rd ch of ch-3, turn.

**Row 3:** Ch 3, dc in same sp; V-st in top of puff st; sk dc, 2 dc in 3rd ch of ch-3, turn.

**Rows 4–15:** Rep [Rows 2 and 3] 6 times.

**Row 16:** Rep Row 2. *(8 puff sts in strip)*

## BORDER

**Rnd 1:** With RS facing and Row 10 at top, ch 3, dc in same ch *(beg cl),* working across Row 10, [ch 1, cl in next ch-1 sp] twice; sk next dc, [cl, ch 4, cl] in next dc, working along side of strip, [ch 1, cl in end of next row] to Row 1; working across end in unused lps of Row 1 [cl, ch 4, cl] in first lp, working across end of strip, [ch 1, cl in sk beg ch] twice, working along other side; [cl, ch 4, cl] in last lp, [ch 1, cl in end of next row] to beg cl, cl in same sp as beg cl, ch 2, join with hdc in top of beg cl. *(16 cls on each side; 4 cls on each end)*

**Rnd 2:** Ch 1, sc in sp formed by joining hdc, *[ch 1, sc in next ch-1 sp] to corner, [sc, ch 4, sc] in corner sp, rep from * around, ending last rep with ch 4; sl st in first sc. Fasten off. *(17 sc on each side; 5 sc on each end)*

## JOINING

Refer to Assembly Diagram for color and placement of squares and rectangles.

To **join blocks**: Finish motifs to the first corner of Rnd 2; sc in corner of working motif; [sl st in corresponding sp of adjacent motif; sk next sc, sc in next ch-1 sp of working motif] across corresponding square and/or rectangle motifs; complete Rnd 2, attaching to other motifs as necessary.

## BORDER

**Rnd 1:** With RS facing and 1 short end at top, attach B in ch-1 sp to left of upper right-hand corner ch-2 sp, ch 3 *(counts as hdc and ch 1-sp),* *[sk next sc, ch 1, hdc in next ch-1 sp] to corner; (hdc, ch 4, hdc) in corner ch-2 sp; rep from * around, ending with sl st in 2nd ch of beg ch-3. Fasten off.

**Rnd 2:** With C, rep Rnd 1.

**Rnd 3:** With D, rep Rnd 1

**Rnd 4:** With E, rep Rnd 1.

**Rnd 5:** Attach A in ch-1 sp after any corner, *ch 4, dc in same sp, sk next dc, next ch-1 sp and next dc, sl st in next ch-1 sp; rep from * around adjusting as necessary to have ch-4 dc lp in corners. Fasten off and weave in all ends. ❧

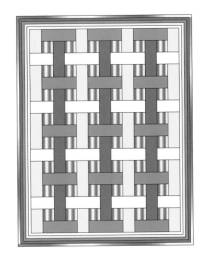

**Spring Plaid**
Assembly Diagram

# LOG CABIN INSPIRATION

Design by Ann E. Smith

## FINISHED SIZE
Approximately 42 x 53 inches

## MATERIALS
- Red Heart Classic medium (worsted) weight yarn (3½ oz/198 yds/99g per skein): 4 skeins each of #853 soft navy (C) and #681 mist green (D)
- Red Heart Kids medium (worsted) weight yarn (5 oz/302 yds/140g per skein): 3 skeins #2850 turquoise (E), 1 skein each of #2734 pink (A) and #2230 yellow (B)
- Size H/8/5mm crochet hook or size needed to obtain gauge

## GAUGE
Motif = 5 inches square

## PATTERN NOTES
To change color at end of row, work until 2 loops of last stitch remain on hook; with new color, yarn over and draw through both loops on hook.

Rounds 1–5 of motif form center square.

## FIRST ROW
### MOTIF A
**Row 1 (RS):** With A, ch 6, sc in 2nd ch from hook and in each rem ch, turn. *(5 sc)*

**Rows 2–4:** Ch 1, sc in each sc, turn.

**Row 5:** Ch 1, sc in each sc, changing to C in last sc, ch 6. Do not turn. Fasten off A. *(center square)*

**Row 6:** Sc in 2nd ch from hook and in next 4 chs, sc in edge sc of next 5 rows along side of center square, turn. *(10 sc)*

**Rows 7–9:** Ch 1, sc in each sc, turn.

**Row 10:** Ch 1, sc in first 9 sc, 3 sc in next sc. Do not turn.

**Row 11:** Working along next side, sc in edge sc of next 3 rows, working in unused lps of beg ch of center square, sc in next 5 lps, turn.

**Row 12:** Ch 1, sc in first 10 sc, turn.

**Rows 13–14:** Ch 1, sc in each sc, turn.

**Row 15:** Ch 1, sc in first 10 sc, changing to D in last sc. Do not turn. Fasten off C.

**Row 16:** Ch 1, working along next side, sc in edge sc of next 5 C rows and 5 A rows, turn. *(10 sc)*

**Rows 17–19:** Ch 1, sc in each sc, turn.

**Row 20:** Ch 1, sc in first 9 sc, 3 sc in next sc. Do not turn.

**Row 21:** Working along next side, sc in edge sc of next 3 D rows, sc in next 5 sts of center square, sl st in first 2 unused lps of C rectangle, turn.

**Row 22:** Ch 1, sk first 2 sl sts, sc in next 10 sc, turn.

**Row 23:** Ch 1, sc in first 10 sc, sl st in next 2 unused lps of C rectangle, turn.

**Row 24:** Rep Row 22.

**Row 25:** Ch 1, sc in first 10 sc, sl st in next unused lp of C rectangle. Fasten off.

***Note:*** *Mark Row 25 as top of motif.*

## BORDER
Hold motif with RS facing and Row 25 at top, join E with sl st in upper right-hand corner, ch 1, (sc, ch 2, sc) in same sp, * work 13 sc along side **, (sc, ch 2, sc) in corner; rep from * 3 times more, ending last rep at **; join with sl st in first sc. Fasten off.

## MOTIF C
Work as for Motif A through Row 25 using B for center square.

## JOINING BORDER
Hold motif with RS facing and Row 25 at top, join E

with sl st in upper right-hand corner, ch 1, (sc, ch 2, sc) in same sp, work 13 sc along next side, (sc, ch 2, sc) in next corner ch-2 sp, work 13 sc along next side, (sc, ch 1) in next corner ch-2 sp, drop lp, insert hook from WS to RS through corresponding corner ch-2 sp of previous motif, draw lp through *(corner joining sp)*, ch 1, sc in same sp on working motif, *ch 1, drop lp, insert hook from WS to RS through corresponding sc on previous motif, draw lp through *(side joining sp)*, ch 1, sc in next sc on working motif; rep from * across skipping 1 sc on previous motif as necessary in order to end with a corner joining sp, work 13 sc along next side, join in first sc. Fasten off.

Referring to Assembly Diagram, alternate Motifs A and C to complete Row 1.

## SECOND ROW
### MOTIF B
**Rows 1–5:** With B, work as for Rows 1–5 of Motif A changing to D at end of Row 5. Fasten off B.
**Rows 6–10:** With D, work as for Rows 6–10 of Motif A.
**Rows 11–14:** Work as Rows 11–14 of Motif A.

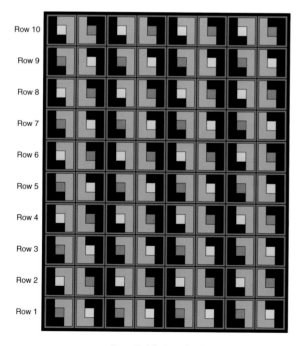

**Log Cabin Inspiration**
Assembly Diagram

**Row 15:** Work as Row 15 of Motif A changing to C in last sc. Fasten off D.
**Row 16:** Ch 1, working along next side, sc in edge sc of next 5 D rows and 5 B rows, turn. *(10 sc)*
**Rows 17–20:** Work same as Rows 17–20 of Motif A.
**Row 21:** Working along next side, sc in edge sc of next 3 C rows, sc in next 5 sts of center square; sl st in first 2 unused lps of D rectangle; turn.
**Rows 22–25:** Work same as Rows 22–25 of Motif A.

## JOINING BORDER
Hold motif with RS facing and Row 25 at top, join E with sl st in upper right-hand corner, ch 1, (sc, ch 2, sc) in same sp, work 13 sc along next side, (sc, ch 1) in next corner, drop lp, insert hook from WS to RS through corresponding corner ch-2 sp of adjacent motif, draw lp through *(corner joining sp)*, ch 1, sc in same sp on working motif, *ch 1, drop lp, insert hook from WS to RS through corresponding sc on adjacent motif, draw lp through *(side joining sp)*, ch 1, sc in next sc on working motif; rep from * across skipping 1 sc on adjacent motif as necessary in order to end with a corner joining sp, work 13 sc along next side, (sc, ch 2, sc) in next corner ch-2 sp, work 13 sc along next side, join in first sc. Fasten off.

## MOTIF D
**Rows 1–5:** Work as for Rows 1–5 of Motif A, changing to D at end of Row 5. Fasten off A.
**Rows 6–25:** Work same as Rows 6–25 of Motif A.

## JOINING BORDER
Hold motif with RS facing, join E with sl st in upper right-hand corner, ch 1, (sc, ch 2, sc) in same sp, work 13 sc along next side, *(sc, ch 1) in next corner, drop lp, insert hook from WS to RS through corresponding corner ch-2 sp of adjacent motif, draw lp through *(corner joining sp)*, ch 1, sc in same sp on working motif, [ch 1, drop lp, insert hook from WS to RS through corresponding sc on adjacent motif, draw lp through *(side joining sp)*, ch 1, sc in next sc on working motif] to next corner skipping 1 sc on adjacent motif

Continued on page 64

# OVERLAPPING SQUARES

Design by Darla Sims

## FINISHED SIZE

Approximately 42 x 58 inches

## MATERIALS

- Red Heart Casual Cot'n Blend (4 oz/140 yds/113g per skein): 6 skeins #3339 majestic (C), 5 skeins each #3937 grand canyon (A) and #3217 creamy (B)
- Size H/8/5mm crochet hook
- Size I/9/5.5mm crochet hook or size needed to obtain gauge

## GAUGE

3 sc = 1 inch
To save time, take time to check gauge.

## PATTERN NOTE

Afghan is worked from right to left in 18 rows.

## FIRST ROW
### FIRST RECTANGLE

**Row 1 (RS):** With larger hook and C, ch 45, sc in 2nd ch from hook and in next 9 chs, sk next 2 chs, sc in next 20 chs, sk next 2 chs, sc in next 10 chs, turn.

**Row 2:** Ch 1, sc in first 9 sc, sk next 2 sc, sc in next 18 sc, sk next 2 sc, sc in next 9 sc, changing to A in last sc, turn.

**Row 3:** Ch 1, sc in first 8 sc, sk next 2 sc, sc in next 16 sc, sk next 2 sc, sc in next 8 sc, changing to B in last sc, turn.

**Row 4:** Ch 1, sc in first 6 sc, sk next 2 sc, sc in next 14 sc, sk next 2 sc, sc in next 6 sc, turn.

**Row 5:** Ch 1, sc in first 4 sc, sk next 2 sc, sc in next 12 sc, sk next 2 sc, sc in next 4 sc, changing to A in last sc, turn.

**Row 6:** Ch 1, sc in first 5 sc, sk next 2 sc, sc in next 10 sc, sk next 2 sc, sc in next 5 sc, changing to C in last sc, turn.

**Row 7:** Ch 1, sc in first 4 sc, sk next 2 sc, sc in next 8 sc, sc in next 4 sc, turn.

**Row 8:** Ch 1, sc in first 3 sc, sk next 2 sc, sc in next 6 sc, sc in next 3 sc, changing to B in last sc, turn.

**Row 9:** Ch 1, sc in first 2 sc, sk next 2 sc, sc in next 4 sc, sc in next 2 sc, changing to A in last sc, turn.

**Row 10:** Ch 1, sc in first sc, sk next 2 sc, sc in next 2 sc, sc in next sc, turn.

**Row 11:** Ch 1, draw up lp in first sc, sk next 2 sc, draw up lp in next sc, yo and draw through all 3 lps on hook. Fasten off.

***Note:*** *Mark Row 11 as top of rectangle.*

## SECOND RECTANGLE

With larger hook and A, ch 34. Fasten off and set aside.

**Row 1:** Attach A in first unused lp in upper left-hand corner of First Rectangle, ch 1, sc in same sp, working in unused lps of beg ch of First Rectangle, sc in next 9 lps, sk next lp and first ch of ch-34, sc in next 20 chs, sk next 2 chs, sc in next 10 chs. Continue as for First Rectangle in following color sequence:

**Rows 2–3:** A; **Row 4:** B; **Rows 5–6:** C; **Rows 7–8:** A; **Rows 9–10:** B; **Row 11:** C.

Referring to Rectangle Color Sequence (page 62) for each rectangle, repeat second rectangle until all 6 rectangles in Row 1 are complete.

## SECOND ROW
## RIGHT HALF RECTANGLE

**Row 1:** With larger hook and B, ch 11, sc in 2nd ch from hook and in next 9 chs, working in edge sc work 10 sc to center of first rectangle on adjacent row, turn. *(20 sc)*

**Row 2:** Ch 1, sc in next 9 sc, sk next 2 sc, sc in next 9 sc, changing to C in last sc, turn.

**Row 3:** Ch 1, sc in next 8 sc, sk next 2 sc, sc in next 8 sc, changing to A in last sc, turn.

**Row 4:** Ch 1, sc in next 7 sc, sk next 2 sc, sc in next 7 sc, turn.

**Row 5:** Ch 1, sc in next 6 sc, sk next 2 sc, sc in next 6 sc, turn.

**Row 6:** Ch 1, sc in next 5 sc, sk next 2 sc, sc in next 5 sc, turn.

**Row 7:** Ch 1, sc in next 4 sc, sk next 2 sc, sc in next 4 sc, changing to B in last sc, turn.

**Row 8:** Ch 1, sc in next 3 sc, sk next 2 sc, sc in next 3 sc, changing to C in last sc, turn.

**Row 9:** Ch 1, sc in next 2 sc, sk next 2 sc, sc in next 2 sc, turn.

**Row 10:** Ch 1, sc in next sc, sk next sc, sc in next sc, changing to B, turn.

**Row 11:** Ch 1, pull up lp in next sc, sk next 2 sc, pull up lp in next sc, yo and draw through all 3 lps on hook. Fasten off.

## RECTANGLE

***Note:*** *Refer to Rectangle Color Sequence for colors.*
With larger hook, join in center of next rectangle on completed row, ch 11. Fasten off.

**Row 1:** Attach indicated color in upper left-hand corner of adjacent rectangle, ch 1, 10 sc along left edge to last row, sk last row and first st on next rectangle on completed row, work 20 sc across rectangles on completed row to ch 11, sk joining and first ch, sc in next 10 chs, turn.

**Rows 2–11:** Work as for Rows 2–11 of First Rectangle referring to Rectangle Color Sequence for colors. Referring to Assembly Diagram for rectangle number and to Rectangle Color Sequence, complete rem rectangles for Row 2.

| | | | | | | |
|---|---|---|---|---|---|---|
| 104 | 103 | 102 | 101 | 100 | 99 | 98 |
| 97 | 96 | 95 | 94 | 93 | 92 | |
| 91 | 90 | 89 | 88 | 87 | 86 | 85 |
| 84 | 83 | 82 | 81 | 80 | 79 | |
| 78 | 77 | 76 | 75 | 74 | 73 | 72 |
| 71 | 70 | 69 | 68 | 67 | 66 | |
| 65 | 64 | 63 | 62 | 61 | 60 | 59 |
| 58 | 57 | 56 | 55 | 54 | 53 | |
| 52 | 51 | 50 | 49 | 48 | 47 | 46 |
| 45 | 44 | 43 | 42 | 41 | 40 | |
| 39 | 38 | 37 | 36 | 35 | 34 | 33 |
| 32 | 31 | 30 | 29 | 28 | 27 | |
| 26 | 25 | 24 | 23 | 22 | 21 | 20 |
| 19 | 18 | 17 | 16 | 15 | 14 | |
| 13 | 12 | 11 | 10 | 9 | 8 | 7 |
| 6 | 5 | 4 | 3 | 2 | 1 | Row 1 |

Start here

**Overlapping Squarez
Assembly Diagram**

## LEFT HALF RECTANGLE

***Note:*** *Refer to Rectangle Color Sequence for colors.*
**Row 1:** Attach indicated color in upper left-hand corner of adjacent rectangle, ch 1, 10 sc along left edge to last row, sk last row and first st on next rectangle on completed row, work 10 sc across rectangle on completed, turn.

**Rows 2–11:** Work as for Rows 2–11 of Right Half Rectangle referring to Rectangle Color Sequence for colors.

## THIRD ROW
## FIRST RECTANGLE

***Note:*** *Refer to Rectangle Color Sequence for colors.*
With larger hook, join color indicated in center of rectangle in completed row, ch 11. Fasten off.

**Row 1:** Ch 11, sc in 2nd ch from hook and in next 9 chs, sk next ch and first st on next rectangle on completed row, work 20 sc across rectangles on completed row to ch 11, sk joining and first ch, sc in next 10 chs, turn.

**Rows 2–11:** Work as for Rows 2–11 of First Rectangle referring to Rectangle Color Sequence for colors. Referring to Assembly Diagram for rectangle number and to Rectangle Color Sequence, complete rem rectangles for Row 3.

## REMAINING RECTANGLES

Referring to Assembly Diagram for rectangle number and to Rectangle Color Sequence below for colors complete rem half rectangles and rectangles.

## BORDER

**Rnd 1:** Hold with 1 short edge at top, with smaller hook, attach B in upper right-hand corner, ch 1, 3 sc in same sp, working around outer edge sc around working 3 sc in each corner; join in first sc.
**Rnd 2:** Ch 1, sc in same sc, sc in each sc working 3 sc in center sc of each corner; join in first sc.
**Rnd 3:** Work same as Rnd 2. Fasten off. Weave in ends.

## RECTANGLE COLOR SEQUENCE

**Rectangle 3:** 2 rows B, 1 row A, 1 row C, 2 rows B, 2 rows A, 3 rows C.

**Rectangle 4:** 1 row C, 2 rows A, 3 rows B, 1 row A, 1 row B, 3 rows C.

**Rectangle 5:** 1 row B, 1 row C, 1 row B, 3 rows A, 2 rows C, 3 rows B.

**Rectangle 6:** 3 rows C, 1 row B, 2 rows A, 1 row B, 4 rows C.

**Rectangle 7:** 2 rows B, 1 row C, 4 rows A, 1 row B, 2 rows C, 1 row B.

**Rectangle 8:** 1 row A, 1 row C, 4 rows B, 1 row C, 4 rows A.

**Rectangle 9:** 1 row A, 2 rows C, 1 row A, 1 row B, 2 rows C, 1 row A, 3 rows B.

**Rectangle 10:** 1 row A, 2 rows B, 1 row A, 4 rows C, 3 rows A.

**Rectangle 11:** 1 row C, 2 rows B, 2 rows A, 3 rows C, 1 row B, 2 rows C.

**Rectangle 12:** 2 rows A, 1 row B, 1 row A, 1 row B, 2 rows C, 2 rows A, 2 rows B.

**Rectangle 13:** 2 rows B, 4 rows C, 1 row A, 2 rows B, 2 rows C.

**Rectangle 14:** 3 rows A, 2 rows B, 2 rows C, 1 row A, 1 row C, 2 rows A.

**Rectangle 15:** 2 rows C, 1 row B, 2 rows A, 1 row B, 1 row A, 2 rows C, 2 rows B.

**Rectangle 16:** 3 rows B, 1 row A, 2 rows C, 1 row B, 4 rows A.

**Rectangle 17:** 2 rows A, 1 row C, 2 rows B, 1 row A, 2 rows B, 1 row C, 2 rows B.

**Rectangle 18:** 1 row C, 4 rows B, 1 row C, 1 row B, 4 rows A.

**Rectangle 19:** 1 row C, 3 rows A, 1 row B, 2 rows C, 1 row A, 3 rows B.

**Rectangle 20:** 1 row B, 2 rows C, 1 row A, 1 row B, 2 rows C, 1 row A, 3 rows B.

**Rectangle 21:** 3 rows C, 4 rows A, 1 row B, 1 row C, 2 rows A.

**Rectangle 22:** 2 rows C, 1 row A, 2 rows C, 1 row B, 2 rows A, 3 rows B.

**Rectangle 23:** 1 row C, 3 rows B, 4 rows A, 1 row B, 2 rows C.

**Rectangle 24:** 2 rows A, 1 row B, 1 row C, 2 rows A, 1 row C, 1 row B, 3 rows A.

**Rectangle 25:** 2 rows B, 1 row C, 1 row A, 2 rows C, 1 row A, 1 row B, 3 rows C.

**Rectangle 26:** 2 rows C, 2 rows A, 1 row B, 1 row C, 5 rows A.

**Rectangle 27:** 4 rows C, 1 row B, 2 rows A, 1 row B, 3 rows C.

**Rectangle 28:** 1 row B, 1 row A, 1 row C, 2 rows B, 2 rows A, 2 rows C, 2 rows B.

**Rectangle 29:** 2 rows C, 3 rows A, 2 rows C, 2 rows B, 2 rows A.

**Rectangle 30:** 1 row B, 1 row C, 1 row A, 3 rows B, 1 row A, 4 rows C.

**Rectangle 31:** 2 rows A, 1 row B, 3 rows C, 1 row B, 1 row A, 1 row B, 2 rows A.

**Rectangle 32:** 2 rows B, 1 row C, 2 rows B, 2 rows A, 1 row B, 3 rows C.

**Rectangle 33:** 3 rows B, 2 rows A, 1 row C, 1 row B, 4 rows A.

**Rectangle 34:** 2 rows C, 1 row B, 2 rows A, 1 row B, 2 rows C, 3 rows B.

**Rectangle 35:** 1 row A, 3 rows B, 1 row C,

1 row B, 1 row A, 1 row B, 1 row C, 2 rows B.

**Rectangle 36:** 3 rows C, 1 row B, 2 rows A, 1 row B, 2 rows C, 2 rows A.

**Rectangle 37:** 4 rows A, 3 rows C, 2 rows B, 2 rows A.

**Rectangle 38:** 1 row C, 2 rows B, 1 row A, 2 rows B, 2 rows C, 1 row B, 1 row A, 1 rows B.

**Rectangle 39:** 3 rows A, 1 row C, 2 rows B, 1 row A, 2 rows C, 2 rows B.

**Rectangle 40:** 1 row C, 3 rows A, 1 row B, 1 row C, 1 row B, 4 rows C.

**Rectangle 41:** 1 row A, 1 row B, 4 rows C, 1 row B, 4 rows A.

**Rectangle 42:** 1 row A, 1 row B, 4 rows C, 1 row B, 4 rows A.

**Rectangle 43:** 3 rows B, 2 row C, 1 row A, 1 row B, 4 rows C.

**Rectangle 44:** 1 row C, 1 row B, 2 rows A, 1 row B, 1 row C, 1 row B, 1 row A, 1 row B, 2 rows C.

**Rectangle 45:** 1 row A, 1 row B, 4 rows C, 1 row B, 1 row A, 3 rows C.

**Rectangle 46:** 2 rows C, 2 rows B, 2 rows A, 2 rows C, 2 rows B, 1 row A.

**Rectangle 47:** 3 rows B, 1 row C, 1 row B, 1 row A, 1 row B, 4 rows C.

**Rectangle 48:** 2 rows C, 2 rows A, 2 rows C, 2 rows A, 3 rows B.

**Rectangle 49:** 2 rows B, 1 row A, 1 row B, 2 rows C, 1 row B, 2 rows A, 2 rows C.

**Rectangle 50:** 3 rows A, 2 rows B, 2 rows C, 1 row B, 3 rows C.

**Rectangle 51:** 3 row A, 2 rows B, 2 rows C, 1 row B, 3 rows C.

**Rectangle 52:** 3 rows B, 1 row A, 2 rows B, 1 row A, 4 rows C.

**Rectangle 53:** 2 rows A, 1 row B, 3 rows C, 1 row B, 2 rows A, 2 rows B.

**Rectangle 54:** 1 row B, 1 row C, 4 rows A, 1 row C, 1 row B, 3 rows A.

**Rectangle 55:** 1 row A, 1 row B, 1 row A, 1 row B, 1 row C, 1 row A, 1 row C, 4 rows B.

**Rectangle 56:** 2 row C, 2 rows A, 3 rows B, 4 rows B.

**Rectangle 57:** 4 rows A, 1 row B, 1 row C, 2 rows A, 1 row B, 2 rows C.

**Rectangle 58:** 1 row C, 1 row B, 1 row A, 3 rows B, 1 row C, 1 row B, 3 rows A.

**Rectangle 59:** 1 row B, 1 row C, 2 rows B, 3 rows A, 3 rows C, 1 row B.

**Rectangle 60:** 4 rows B, 1 row A, 2 rows B, 1 row C, 3 rows B.

**Rectangle 61:** 2 rows C, 2 rows A, 1 row B, 2 rows A, 1 row B, 1 row C, 2 rows B.

**Rectangle 62:** 1 row A, 2 rows B, 2 rows C, 1 row B, 2 rows C, 3 rows A.

**Rectangle 63:** 1 row B, 1 row A, 1 row C, 1 row A, 1 row B, 1 row A, 1 row C, 1 row A, 3 rows B.

**Rectangle 64:** 2 rows C, 3 rows B, 2 rows A, 1 row B, 3 rows C.

**Rectangle 65:** 2 rows A, 4 rows C, 1 row B, 4 rows A.

**Rectangle 66:** 1 row A, 2 rows C, 1 row A, 1 row B, 1 row A, 2 rows C, 1 row A, 2 rows B.

**Rectangle 67:** 1 row C, 2 rows B, 3 rows A, 5 rows C.

**Rectangle 68:** 1 row A, 1 row B, 2 rows C, 1 row A, 1 row B, 2 rows C, 1 row A, 2 rows B.

**Rectangle 69:** 1 row B, 1 row A, 1 row B, 1 row A, 3 rows C, 1 row B, 3 rows A.

**Rectangle 70:** 2 rows C, 2 rows B, 2 rows C, 2 rows B, 3 rows A.

**Rectangle 71:** 1 row B, 4 rows A, 2 rows C, 1 row B, 1 row A, 1 row C, 1 row B.

**Rectangle 72:** 3 rows C, 3 rows B, 5 rows A.

**Rectangle 73:** 2 rows B, 1 row A, 1 row C, 2 rows B, 1 row A, 1 row C, 3 rows B.

**Rectangle 74:** 2 rows C, 1 row A, 1 row B, 3 rows C, 4 rows A.

**Rectangle 75:** 1 row A, 4 rows B, 1 row A, 1 row B, 4 rows C.

**Rectangle 76:** 2 rows C, 2 rows B, 2 rows C, 2 rows A, 3 rows B.

**Rectangle 77:** 2 rows A, 1 row B, 1 row C, 1 row B, 1 row A, 1 row B, 1 row C, 3 rows A.

**Rectangle 78:** 3 rows B, 2 rows C, 2 rows B, 1 row A, 3 rows B.

**Rectangle 79:** 2 rows A, 1 row B, 2 rows C, 1 row B, 2 rows C, 1 row B, 2 rows A.

**Rectangle 80:** 2 row C, 3 rows B, 1 row A, 2 rows B, 3 rows C.

**Rectangle 81:** 1 row B, 4 rows A, 1 row B, 1 row C, 1 row B, 1 row C, 2 rows B.

**Rectangle 82:** 1 row C, 2 rows B, 1 row A, 2 rows C, 2 rows B, 1 row A, 2 rows C.

**Rectangle 83:** 4 rows B, 1 row A, 1 row B, 1 row D, 4 rows A.

**Rectangle 84:** 3 rows C, 1 row B, 3 rows A, 4 rows B.

**Rectangle 85:** 1 row B, 3 rows C, 3 rows A, 1 row B, 3 rows C.

**Rectangle 86:** 2 rows A, 1 row B, 1 row C, 1 row B, 2 rows A, 1 row B, 1 row C, 2 rows B.

**Rectangle 87:** 2 rows B, 4 rows C, 2 rows B, 3 rows A.

**Rectangle 88:** 2 rows A, 4 rows B, 5 rows C.

**Rectangle 89:** 2 rows C, 1 row B, 3 rows A, 2 rows C, 1 row B, 2 rows A.

**Rectangle 90:** 1 row B, 1 row C, 1 row B, 1 row C, 1 row B, 1 row A, 5 rows B.

**Rectangle 91:** 2 rows C, 2 rows B, 4 rows A, 3 rows C.

**Rectangle 92:** 1 row C, 4 rows B, 1 row C, 2 rows B, 3 rows A.

**Rectangle 93:** 1 row B, 1 row A, 1 row C, 1 row A, 1 row B, 1 row A, 1 row C, 1 row A, 3 rows B.

**Rectangle 94:** 1 row C, 3 rows A, 2 rows B, 1 row C, 4 rows A.

**Rectangle 95:** 1 row B, 2 rows C, 1 row B, 1 row A, 2 rows C, 1 row B, 1 row C, 2 rows B.

**Rectangle 96:** 4 rows C, 2 rows A, 1 row C, 2 rows A, 2 rows C.

**Rectangle 97:** 2 rows A, 2 rows B, 1 row C, 1 row B, 2 rows A, 3 rows B.

**Rectangle 98:** 1 row B, 2 rows A, 1 row B, 2 rows C, 1 row B, 1 row C, 3 rows B.

**Rectangle 99:** 1 row C, 2 rows A, 1 row C, 2 rows A, 1 row B, 1 row C, 1 row B, 2 rows C.

**Rectangle 100:** 3 rows B, 1 row C, 3 rows B, 4 rows A.

**Rectangle 101:** 2 rows C, 1 row B, 2 rows A, 1 row C, 2 rows A, 1 row B, 2 rows C.

**Rectangle 102:** 2 rows B, 1 row A, 4 rows C, 1 row A, 3 rows B.

**Rectangle 103:** 1 row C, 1 row B, 3 rows A, 1 row B, 1 row A, 1 row B, 1 row A, 2 rows C.

**Rectangle 104:** 1 row A, 3 rows C, 1 row B, 6 rows A. 🐾

# LOG CABIN INSPIRATION Continued from page 58

as necessary in order to end with a corner joining sp; rep from * once more, (sc, ch 1) in next corner, drop lp, insert hook from WS to RS through corresponding corner ch-2 sp of adjacent motif, draw lp through *(corner joining sp)*, ch 1, sc in same sp on working motif, work 13 sc along next side, join in first sc.

Referring to Assembly Diagram, alternate Motifs B and D to complete row 2.

Referring to Assembly Diagram, alternate Rows 1 and 2 until 8 rows are joined.

## BORDER

**Rnd 1:** With RS facing, attach E in upper right-hand corner ch-2 sp, ch 1, (sc, ch 2, sc) in same sp, *[sc in next 15 sc, sc in next 2 ch-2 sps] 8 times, sc in next 15 sc, (sc, ch 2, sc) in corner ch-2 sp, [sc in next 15 sc, sc in next 2 ch-2 sps] 9 times, sc in 15 sc**, (sc, ch 2, sc) in corner ch-2 sp, rep from * ending at **; join with sl st in first sc.

**Rnd 2:** Ch 1, sc in same sc as joining; * working from left to right, ch 2, sk next sc, sc in next sc; rep from * around, join with sl st in first sc. Fasten off.

**Rnd 3:** With RS facing, join C with sl st in any ch-2 sp, ch 1, sc in same sp, * working from left to right, ch 2, sc in next ch-2 sp; rep from * around.

**Rnd 4:** * Working from left to right, ch 2, sc in next ch-2 sp; rep from * around, ending ch 2, sl st in first ch-2 sp. Fasten off and weave in all ends. 🐾

# FURRY FRENZY

Definitely not your usual afghans, these designs have some furry or fuzzy yarn added to the mix. What a great way to use those new yarns!

# BURSTS OF FUR

Design by Tammy Hildebrand

## FINISHED SIZE
Approximately 44 x 58 inches

## MATERIALS
- Lion Brand Homespun bulky (chunky) weight yarn (6 oz/185 yds/170g per skein): 3 skeins #346 bella vista (A)
- Lion Brand Fancy Fur novelty yarn (1.75 oz/39 yds/ 50g per skein): 7 skeins #255 jungle print (B)
- Size N/13/9mm crochet hook or size needed to obtain gauge

## GAUGE
Motif = 13 inches square
To save time, take time to check gauge.

## SPECIAL STITCHES
For **joining ch-3 sp:** Ch 1, drop lp, insert hook in 2nd ch of corresponding ch-3 on adjacent motif, pick up dropped lp and draw through, ch 1.

For **joining ch-5 sp:** Ch 2, drop lp, insert hook in 3rd ch of corresponding ch-5 on adjacent motif, pick up dropped lp and draw through, ch 2.

## PATTERN NOTES
Join with a slip stitch unless otherwise stated.
Fancy Fur is added after motif is completed.

## FIRST MOTIF
**Rnd 1:** With A, ch 4, join to form ring, ch 4 (counts as dc and ch-1 sp), [dc in ring, ch 1] 7 times, join in first sc.

**Rnd 2:** Sl st in next ch-1 sp, ch 3, (2 dc, ch 2, 3 dc) in next ch-1 sp, *dc in next ch-1 sp, (3 dc, ch 2, 3 dc) in next ch-1 sp; rep from * twice more, join in 3rd ch of beg ch-3.

**Rnd 3:** Ch 3, dc in next 2 sts, *(2 dc, ch 2, 2 dc) in next ch-2 sp, dc in next 7 sts; rep from * twice more, (2 dc, ch 2, 2 dc) in next ch-2 sp, dc in next 4 sts, join in 3rd ch of beg ch-3.

**Rnd 4:** Sl st in next st, ch 4, (counts as dc and ch-1 sp), sk next st, dc in next st, ch 1, *(dc, ch 3, dc) in next ch-2 sp, [ch 1, sk next st, dc in next st] 5 times, ch 1; rep from * twice more, (dc, ch 3, dc) in next ch-2 sp, [ch 1, sk next st, dc in next st] 3 times, ch 1, join with sl st in 3rd ch of beg ch-4.

**Rnd 5:** Ch 3, dc in each st and ch-1 sp to next ch-3 sp, *(dc, ch 2, dc) in next ch-3 sp, dc in each st and ch-1 sp to next ch-3 sp; rep from * twice more, (dc, ch 2, dc) in next ch-3 sp, dc in each st and ch-1 sp to beg ch-3, join in 3rd ch of beg ch-3.

**Rnd 6:** Ch 6 (counts as a dc and ch-3 sp), dc in same st [sk next st, (dc, ch 3, dc) in next st] twice, *(dc, ch 3, dc, ch 5, dc, ch 3, dc) in next corner ch-2 sp, [sk next st, (dc, ch 3, dc) in next st] 7 times; rep from * twice more, (dc, ch 3, dc, ch 5, dc, ch 3, dc) in next ch-2 sp, [sk next st, (dc, ch 3, dc) in next st] 4 times, join in first sc. Fasten off.

## SECOND MOTIF
Referring to Assembly Diagram, work same as Rnds 1–5 of First Motif.

**Rnd 6 (joining rnd):** Ch 6 (counts as a dc and ch-3 sp), dc in same st [sk next st, (dc, ch 3, dc) in next st) twice, (dc, ch 3, dc, **joining ch-5 sp** {see Special Stitches}, dc, **joining ch-3 sp** {see Special Stitches}, dc) in next corner ch-2 sp, [sk next st, (dc, joining ch-3 sp, dc) in next st] 7 times, (dc, joining ch-3 sp, dc, joining ch-5 sp, dc, ch 3, dc) in next corner ch-2 sp, *[sk next st, (dc, ch 3, dc) in next st] 7 times, (dc, ch 3, dc, ch 5, dc, ch 3, dc) in next corner ch-2 sp; rep from * once more, [sk next st, (dc, ch 3, dc) in next st] 4 times; join in first sc. Fasten off.

## REMAINING MOTIFS

Referring to Assembly Diagram, work rem motifs as for Second Motif. Join to adjacent motifs in similar manner, making sure all 4-corner joinings are secure.

## FUR TRIM

Working around **posts** (see Stitch Guide) of dc on Rnd 1, join B with sc around any st, (dc, sc) around same st, ch 1, *(sc, dc, sc, ch 1) around post of next dc; rep from * around, join in first sc. Fasten off. Rep Fur Trim around post of dc of rnd 4.

## BORDER

**Rnd 1:** Hold with RS facing and one short end at top, join A with sc in ch-5 sp in upper right-hand corner, 2 sc in same sp, *[3 dc in each of next 9 ch-3 sp, 3 tr in center of block joining] twice, 3 dc in each of next 9 ch-3 sps, 3 sc in next ch-5 sp, [3 dc in each of next 9 ch-3 sp, 3 tr in center of block joining] 3 times, 3 dc in each of next 9 ch-3 sps**, 3 sc in next ch-5 sp; rep from * ending at **, join in first sc.

**Rnd 2:** Ch 3, (2 dc, ch 1, 2 dc) in next sc, dc in each st to 2nd sc of next corner 3-sc group, *(2 dc, ch 1, 2 dc) in next ch-1 sp, dc in each st to 2nd sc of next corner 3-sc group; rep from * twice more, dc in each st to beg ch-3; join in 3rd ch of beg ch-3. Fasten off.

**Rnd 3:** Attach B with sl st in any st, sl st in each st and ch-1 sp around.

Fasten off and weave in all ends. 🐾

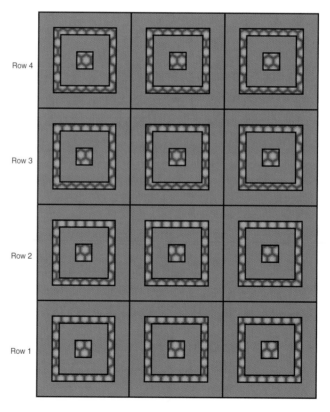

**Bursts of Fur**
Assembly Diagram

**SKILL LEVEL**
INTERMEDIATE

**YARN WEIGHT**
5 BULKY

# LUSCIOUS LIMES

Design by Tammy Hildebrand

## FINISHED SIZE
Approximately 43 x 59 inches

## MATERIALS
- Lion Brand Homespun bulky (chunky) weight yarn (6 oz/185 yds/170g per ball): 5 balls #369 Florida key green (A)
- Lion Brand Fun Fur novelty yarn (1.75 oz/60 yds/50g per ball): 6 balls #207 citrus (B)
- Size N/13/9mm crochet hook or size needed to obtain gauge

## GAUGE
Motif =14½ inches square
To save time, take time to check gauge.

## SPECIAL STITCHES
For **front post double crochet (fpdc):** Yo, insert hook from front to back to front around **post** *(see Stitch Guide)* of st indicated, draw up lp, [yo and draw through 2 lps on hook] twice.

For **cross stitch (cross st):** Sk next st, dc in next st, working over st just made, dc in skipped st.

For **joining ch-3 sp:** Ch 1, drop lp from hook, insert hook in 2nd ch of corresponding ch-3 sp on adjacent motif, pick up dropped lp and draw through.

For **joining ch-5 sp:** Ch 2, drop lp from hook, insert hook in 3rd ch of corresponding ch-5 sp on adjacent motif, pick up dropped lp and draw through.

## PATTERN NOTE
Join with a slip stitch unless otherwise stated.

## FIRST MOTIF
**Rnd 1:** With A, ch 4, join to form ring, ch 3 *(counts as dc),* 2 dc in ring, ch 2, [3 dc in ring, ch 2] 3 times, join in 3rd ch of beg ch-3.

**Rnd 2:** Ch 4, *(counts as dc and a ch-1 sp),* sk next dc, dc in next dc, *(2 dc, ch 2, 2 dc) in next ch-2 sp *(corner),* dc in next dc, ch 1, sk next dc, dc in next dc; rep from * twice more, (2 dc, ch 2, 2 dc) in next ch-2 sp *(corner),* join in 3rd ch of beg ch-4. Fasten off.

**Rnd 3:** Attach B in any corner ch-2 sp, ch 3 *(counts as dc),* 4 dc in same sp, ch 3, 5 dc in next ch-1 sp *(shell),* ch 3, [5 dc in next ch-2 sp *(shell),* ch 3, 5 dc in next ch-1 sp *(shell),* ch 3] 3 times, join in 3rd ch of beg ch-3. Fasten off.

**Rnd 4:** Working over ch-2 sp of Rnd 3, attach A in dc of Rnd 2 before any corner shell, ch 6, *(counts as dc and ch-3 sp),* sk next shell, *working over next ch-2 sp, dc in next 3 dc of Rnd 2, ch 1, sk next shell**, working over next ch-2 sp, dc in next 3 dc of Rnd 2, ch 3, sk next shell; rep from * 3 times more, ending last rep at **; working over next ch-2 sp, dc in next 2 dc, join in 3rd ch of beg ch-6.

**Rnd 5:** Ch 3, *(2 dc, ch 2, 2 dc) in next ch-3 sp, dc in next 3 sts, dc in next ch-1 sp**, dc in next 3 sts, rep from * 3 times more, ending last rep at **, dc in next ch-1 sp, dc in last 2 sts, join in 3rd ch of beg ch-3.

**Rnd 6:** Sl st in next dc, ch 4, *(dc, ch 2, dc) in next corner ch-2 sp, ch 1, [sk next st, dc in next st, ch 1] 5 times; rep from * twice more, (dc, ch 2, dc) in next corner ch-2 sp, ch 1, [sk next st, dc in next st, ch 1] 4 times, join in 3rd ch of beg ch-4. Fasten off.

**Rnd 7:** Attach B around **post** *(see Stitch Guide)* of any dc on Rnd 6, ch 5, *(counts as dc and a ch-2 sp),* **fpdc** *(see Special Stitches)* around same st, ch 3, *(fpdc, ch 2, fpdc) around post of next st, ch 3; rep around, join in 3rd ch of beg ch-5. Fasten off.

**Rnd 8:** Working behind Rnd 7, attach A in any corner ch-2 sp of Rnd 6, ch 3, dc in same sp, sc in corresponding ch-3 sp of Rnd 7, 2 dc in same corner ch-2 sp of Rnd 6, sc in next ch-3 sp of Rnd 7, [2 dc in next ch-1 sp of Rnd 6, sc in next ch-3 sp of Rnd 7] 6 times, *2 dc in next corner ch-2 sp of Rnd 6, sc in corner ch-3 sp of Rnd 7, 2 dc in same corner ch-2 sp of Rnd 6, [2 dc in next ch-1 sp of Rnd 6, sc in next ch-3 sp of Rnd 7] 6 times; rep from * twice more, join in 3rd ch of beg ch-3.

**Rnd 9:** Sl st in next st, ch 3, working over ch-3, dc in previous st, *(dc, ch 2, dc) in next sc *(corner)*, [**cross-st** *(see Special Stitches)* over next 2 dc] twice, [sk next sc, cross-st over next 2 dc] 6 times; rep from * twice more, (dc, ch 2, dc) in next sc *(corner)*, [cross-st over next 2 dc] twice, [sk next sc, cross-st over next 2 dc] 5 times join in 3rd ch of beg ch-3.

**Rnd 10:** Ch 1, sc in same ch as joining, ch 3, sk next cross-st, sc in sp before next dc, *(sc, ch 3, sc, ch 5, sc, ch 3, sc) in corner ch-2 sp, sk next st, [sc in sp before next cross-st, ch 3, sk next cross-st] 8 times, sc in sp before next dc; rep from * twice more, (sc, ch 3, sc, ch 5, sc, ch 3, sc) in next ch-2 sp, sk next st, [sc in sp before next cross-st, ch 3, sk next cross-st] 7 times, join in first sc. Fasten off.

## SECOND MOTIF

Work same as Rnds 1–9 of First Motif.

**Rnd 10 (joining rnd):** Ch 1, sc in same sp as joining, ch 3, sk next cross-st, sc in sp before next dc, (sc, ch 3, sc, **joining ch-5 sp** *{see Special Stitches}*, sc, **joining ch-3 sp** *{see Special Stitches}*, sc) in corner ch-2 sp, sk next st, [sc in sp before next cross-st, joining ch-3 sp, sk next cross-st] 8 times, sc in sp before next st, (sc, joining ch-3 sp, sc, joining ch-5 sp, sc, ch 3, sc) in corner ch-2 sp, *sk next st, [sc in sp before next cross-st, ch 3, sk next cross-st] 8 times, (sc, ch 3, sc, ch 5, sc, ch 3, sc) in next ch-2 sp; rep from * once more, sk next st, [sc in sp before next cross-st, ch 3, sk next cross-st] 7 times, join in first sc. Fasten off.

## REMAINING MOTIFS

Referring to Assembly Diagram for placement, work same as for Second Motif, joining to adjacent motifs in similar manner.

## BORDER

*Note: For **dec**, draw up lp in each of 2 sts indicated, yo and draw through all 3 lps on hook.*

Hold with RS facing and one short end at top, attach A with sc in upper right-hand corner ch-5 sp, (ch 3, sc, ch 5, sc, ch 3, sc) in same sp, *[sc in next ch-3 sp, ch 3] 8 times, sc in next ch-3 sp, (sc, ch 3, sc) in next corner ch-5 sp, ch 3, **dec** *(see Note)* over next dc and corresponding dc on next motif, ch 3, (sc, ch 3, sc) in next corner ch-5 sp work, rep from * to next outer corner, (sc, ch 3, sc, ch 5, sc, ch 3, sc) in corner ch-5 sp, work in similar manner around; join in first sc.

Fasten off and weave in ends. 🦃

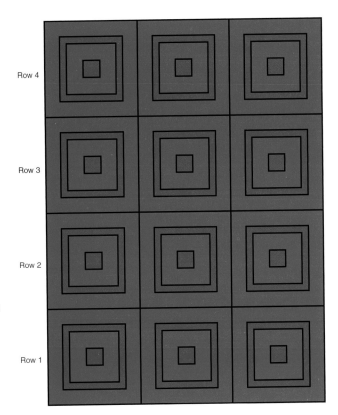

**Luscious Limes**
Assembly Diagram

# VELVETY ROSES

Design by Tammy Hildebrand

## FINISHED SIZE
Approximately 42 x 62 inches

## MATERIALS
- Lion Brand Chenille Thick & Quick super bulky yarn (100 yds per skein): 1 skein each #157 lemon yellow (A), #191 violet (B), #112 raspberry (C) and #148 turquoise (D)
- Lion Brand Wool-Ease bulky (chunky) weight yarn (5 oz/153 yds/140g per ball): 5 balls each #130 grass (E), #099 fisherman (F)
- Size P/15/10mm crochet hook or size needed to obtain gauge

## GAUGE
Motif = 10½ inches square
To save time, take time to check gauge.

## SPECIAL STITCHES
For **cluster (cl):** Keeping last lp of each dc on hook 2 dc in st or sp indicated, yo and draw through all 3 lps on hook.

For **joining ch-3 sp:** Ch 1, drop lp, insert hook in 2nd ch of corresponding ch-3 sp on adjacent motif, pick up dropped lp and draw through, ch 1.

For **joining ch-5 sp:** Ch 2, drop lp, insert hook in 3rd ch of corresponding ch-5 sp on adjacent motif, pick up dropped lp and draw through, ch 2.

## PATTERN NOTE
Join with a slip stitch unless otherwise stated.

## FIRST MOTIF
**Rnd 1:** With A, ch 4 join to form a ring, ch 3, keeping last lp on hook, dc in ring, yo and draw through both lps on hook, (beg-cl), ch 1, [**cl** (see Special Stitches) in ring, ch 1] 7 times, join in top of beg-cl.

**Rnd 2:** Ch 1, sc in top of same cl, 3 dc in next ch-1 sp, [sc in next cl, 3 dc in next ch-1 sp] 7 times, join in first sc.

**Rnd 3:** Ch 1, working behind Rnd 2 around **posts** (see Stitch Guide) of cls on Rnd 1, sc around post of first cl, ch 2, [sc around next cl, ch 2] 7 times, join in first-sc. Fasten off.

**Rnd 4:** Attach E in any ch-2 sp, ch 3, (dc, ch 2, 2 dc) in same sp (corner), 3 dc in next ch-2 sp, *(2 dc, ch 2, 2 dc) in next ch-2 sp (corner), 3 dc in next ch-2 sp; rep from * twice more, join in 3rd ch of beg ch-3.

**Rnd 5:** Ch 1, (sc, ch 3, sc) in same ch as joining, *(sc, ch 3, sc) in next ch-2 sp, sk next 2 sts, (sc, ch 3, sc) in sp before next st, sk next st, (sc, ch 3, sc) in next st, sk next st, (sc, ch 3, sc) in sp before next st; rep from * twice more, (sc, ch 3, sc) in next ch-2 sp, sk next 2 sts, (sc, ch 3, sc) in sp before next st, sk next st, (sc, ch 3, sc) in next st, join in first sc. Fasten off.

**Rnd 6:** Attach F in any corner ch-3 sp, ch 3, (2 dc, ch 2, 3 dc) in same sp, *(dc, ch 1, dc) in next ch-3 sp, sc in next ch-3 sp, (dc, ch 1, dc) in next ch-3 sp, (3 dc, ch 2, 3 dc) in next ch-3 sp; rep from * twice more, (dc, ch 1, dc) in next ch-3 sp, sc in next ch-3 sp, (dc, ch 1, dc) in next ch-3 sp, join in 3rd ch of beg ch-3.

**Rnd 7:** Sl st in next st, ch 4, dc in same st, *5 dc in next ch-2 sp, sk next st, (dc, ch 1, dc) in next st, dc in next ch-1 sp, 3 dc in next sc, dc in next ch-1 sp, sk next 2 sts, (dc, ch 1, dc) in next st; rep from * twice more, 5 dc in next ch-2 sp, sk next st, (dc, ch 1, dc) in next st, dc in next ch-1 sp, 3 dc in next sc, dc in next ch-1 sp, join 3rd ch of beg ch-4. Fasten off.

**Rnd 8:** Attach E with a sc in 3rd dc of any 5-dc corner, ch 3, sc in same st, *sk next st, (sc, ch 3, sc) in next st, (sc, ch 3, sc) in next ch-1 sp, [sk next st,

(sc, ch 3, sc) in next st] 3 times, (sc, ch 3, sc) in next ch-1 sp, sk next st, (sc, ch 3, sc) in next st, (sc, ch 3, sc, ch 5, sc, ch 3, sc) in next st; rep from * twice more, sk next st, (sc, ch 3, sc) in next st, (sc, ch 3, sc) in next ch-1 sp, [sk next st, (sc, ch 3, sc) in next st] 3 times, (sc, ch 3, sc) in next ch-1 sp, sk next st, (sc, ch 3, sc) in next st, (sc, ch 3, sc) in beg corner, join in first-sc. Fasten off.

```
COLOR KEY
▢ Lemon Yellow
■ Violet
■ Raspberry
■ Turquoise
```

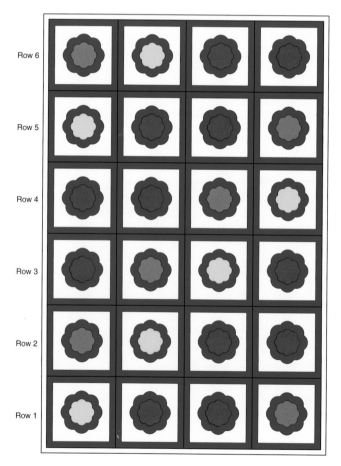

**Velvet Roses**
Assembly Diagram

## SECOND MOTIF

Referring to Assembly Diagram for color and placement, work same as Rnds 1–7 of First Motif.
**Rnd 8:** Attach E with sc in 3rd dc of any 5-dc corner group, ch 3, sc in same st, **joining ch-5 sp** *(see Special Stitches)*, [sc, **joining ch-3 sp** *(see Special Stitches),* sc] in same st, sk next st, (sc, joining ch-3, sc) in next st, (sc, joining ch-3, sc) in next ch-1 sp, [sk next st, (sc, joining ch-3, sc) in next st] 3 times, (sc, joining ch-3, sc) in next ch-1 sp, sk next st, (sc, joining ch-3, sc) in next st, joining ch-5, (sc, ch 3, sc) in same st, *sk next st, (sc, ch 3, sc) in next st, (sc, ch 3, sc) in next ch-1 sp, [sk next st, (sc, ch 3, sc) in next st] 3 times, (sc, ch 3, sc) in next ch-1 sp, sk next st, (sc, ch 3, sc) in next st, (sc, ch 3, sc, ch 5, sc, ch 3, sc) in next st; rep from * once more, sk next st, (sc, ch 3, sc) in next st, (sc, ch 3, sc) in next ch-1 sp, [sk next st, (sc, ch 3, sc) in next st] 3 times, (sc, ch 3, sc) in next ch-1 sp, sk next st, (sc, ch 3, sc) in next st, join in first sc. Fasten off.

## REMAINING MOTIFS

Referring to Assembly Diagram for color and placement, work rem motifs as for Second Motif, joining to adjacent motifs in similar manner and making sure all 4-corner joinings are secure.

## BORDER

Hold with RS facing and one short end at top, attach F with sc in ch-5 sp in upper right-hand corner, 3 sc in same sp, *[(sc in next ch-3 sp, 4 sc in next ch-3 sp) 4 times, sc in next ch-3 sp, 3 dc in center of motif joining] 3 times, [sc in next ch-3 sp, 4 sc in next ch-3 sp] 4 times, sc in next ch-3 sp, 4 sc in next ch-5, [{sc in next ch-3 sp, 4 sc in next ch-3 sp} 4 times, sc in next ch-3 sp, 3 dc in center of motif joining] 5 times, [sc in next ch-3 sp, 4 sc in next ch-3 sp] 4 times, sc in next ch-3 sp**, 4 sc in next ch-5 sp; rep from * ending at **, join in first sc.
Fasten off and weave in all ends. ❧

# BEBOP BLOCKS

Design by Tammy Hildebrand

## FINISHED SIZE
Approximately 48 x 65 inches

## MATERIALS
- Bernat Soft Bouclé bulky (chunky) weight yarn (5 oz/255 yds/140g per ball): 9 balls #26515 softest straw (A)
- Patons Cha-Cha (1.75 oz/77 yds/50g per ball): 6 balls #02004 salsa (B)
- Size P/15/10mm crochet hook or size needed to obtain gauge

## GAUGE
Motif = 12 inches square
To save time, take time to check gauge.

## SPECIAL STITCHES
For **cross-stitch (cross-st):** Sk next dc, dc in next dc, working over st just made, dc in skipped st.

For **joining ch-3 sp:** Ch 1, drop lp from hook, insert hook in 2nd ch of corresponding ch-3 on adjacent motif, pick up dropped lp and draw through, ch 1.

For **joining ch-5 sp:** Ch 2, drop lp from hook, insert hook in 3rd ch of corresponding ch-5 on adjacent motif, pick up dropped lp and draw through, ch 2.

## PATTERN NOTE
Join with a slip stitch unless otherwise stated.

## FIRST MOTIF
**Rnd 1:** With 2 strands A held tog, ch 4, join to form ring, ch 4 (counts as dc and ch-1 sp), [dc in ring, ch 1] 7 times, join in 3rd ch of beg ch-4. Fasten off.

**Rnd 2:** Attach B with sc in any dc, 3 dc in next ch-1 sp, [sc in next dc, 3 dc in next ch-1 sp] 7 times, join in first sc. Fasten off.

**Rnd 3:** Attach 2 strands A with sc around **post** (see Stitch Guide) of any dc on rnd 1, ch 3, [sc around post of next dc on rnd 1, ch 3] 7 times, join in first sc.

**Rnd 4:** Sl st in next ch-3 sp, ch 3, (dc, ch 3, 2 dc) in same sp (corner), *2 dc in next ch-3 sp, (2 dc, ch 3, 2 dc) in next ch-3 sp; rep from * twice more, 2 dc in next ch-3 sp, join in 3rd ch of beg ch-3.

**Rnd 5:** Sl st in next dc and in next ch-3 sp, ch 3, (dc, ch 2, 2 dc) in same sp, **cross-st** (see Special Stitches), *[cross-st over next 2 sts] twice, (2 dc, ch 2, 2 dc) in next ch-3 sp, cross-st, rep from * twice more, [cross-st over next 2 sts] twice, join in 3rd ch of beg ch-3.

**Rnd 6:** Working in **back lps** only, ch 3, dc in next st, *(dc, ch 2, dc) in next ch-2 sp, dc in each st to next corner ch-2 sp; rep from * twice more, join in 3rd ch of beg ch-3.

**Rnd 7:** Ch 6 (counts as dc and ch-3 sp), dc in same sp as joining, *(dc, ch 3, dc, ch 5, dc, ch 3, dc) in next ch-2 sp, [sk next 2 sts, (dc, ch 3, dc) in sp before next st] 5 times; rep from * twice more, (dc, ch 3, dc, ch 5, dc, ch 3, dc) in next ch-2 sp, [sk next 2 sts, (dc, ch 3, dc) in sp before next st] 4 times, join in 3rd ch of beg ch-6. Fasten off.

## SECOND MOTIF
Referring to Assembly Diagram for placement, work same as Rnds 1–6 of First Motif.

**Rnd 7 (joining rnd):** Ch 6, dc in same sp as joining, (dc, ch 3, dc, **joining ch-5 sp** {see Special Stitches}, dc, **joining ch-3 sp** {see Special Stitches}, dc) in next ch-2 sp, [sk next 2 sts, (dc, joining ch-3 sp, dc) in sp before next st] 5 times, (dc, joining ch-3 sp, dc, joining ch-5 sp, dc, ch 3, dc) in next ch-2 sp, *[sk next 2 sts, (dc, ch 3, dc) in sp before next st] 5 times, (dc, ch 3, dc, ch 5, dc, ch 3, dc) in next ch-2 sp; rep from * once more, [sk next 2 sts, (dc, ch 3, dc) in sp before next st] 4 times, join in 3rd ch of beg ch-6. Fasten off.

## REMAINING MOTIFS

Referring to Assembly Diagram for placement, work rem motifs in same manner as Second Motif, joining to adjacent motifs in similar manner and making sure all 4-corner joinings are secure.

## MOTIF TRIM

Working in unused front lps of Rnd 5, attach B with sc in first ch of any corner, working between sts of Rnd 7, 3 dc between center sts, sc in next unused lp of Rnd 5, *[sc in next unused lp of Rnd 5, 3 dc between

2 sts directly above on Rnd 7, sc in next unused lp of Rnd 5] 5 times, sc in next unused lp of Rnd 5, 3 dc between center sts of next corner; rep from * twice more, [sc in next unused lp of Rnd 5, 3 dc between 2 sts directly above on Rnd 7, sc in next unused lp of Rnd 5] 5 times, join in first sc. Fasten off.

## BORDER

Hold with RS facing and one short edge at top, attach 2 strands of A with sl st in ch-5 sp in upper right-hand corner, ch 3, 4 dc in same sp, sc in next ch-3 sp, *5 dc in next ch-3 sp or motif joining, sc in next ch-3 sp; rep from * around, join in 3rd ch of beg ch-3. Fasten off and weave in all ends. 🐾

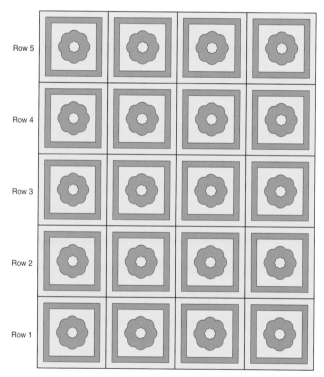

**Bebop Blocks**
Assembly Diagram

# MYSTICAL MIST

Design by Darla Sims

## FINISHED SIZE

Approximately 48 x 62 inches including border

## MATERIALS

- Bernat Satin medium (worsted) weight yarn (3.5 oz/ 163 yds/100g per ball): 7 balls #04007 silk (A), 4 balls #04141 sapphire (C)
- Bernat Eyelash novelty yarn (1.75 oz/77 yds/50g per ball): 4 balls #35142 hip (B)
- Bernat Ping Pong super bulky (bulky) weight yarn (1.75 oz/58 yds/50g per ball): 3 balls #51134 blazing blue (D)
- Size G/6/4mm crochet hook
- Size H/8/5mm crochet hook or size needed to obtain gauge

## GAUGE

Motif = 7½ inches square
To save time, take time to check gauge.

## PATTERN NOTE

Join with a slip stitch unless otherwise stated.

## FIRST ROW
## FIRST MOTIF

**Rnd 1:** With larger hook and D, ch 5, join to form a ring, ch 3 *(counts as dc)* 15 dc in ring; join in 3rd ch of beg ch-3. Fasten off. *(16 dc)*

**Rnd 2:** Attach A in any st, ch 6 *(counts as tr and ch-2 sp)*, [tr in next st, ch 2] 15 times, ch 2; join in 4th ch of beg ch-6. Fasten off.

**Rnd 3:** Attach B in any ch-2 sp, ch 3, 2 dc in next ch-2 sp, [3 dc in next ch-2 sp, ch 3] 15 times, join in 3rd ch of beg ch-3. Fasten off.

**Rnd 4:** Attach A in any ch-3 sp, ch 1, sc in same sp, [ch 3, sc in next ch-3 sp] 3 times, *ch 5 *(corner)*, [sc in next ch-3 sp, ch 3] 3 times, sc in next ch-3 sp; rep from * twice more, ch 5; join in first sc. Fasten off.

**Rnd 5:** Attach C in any corner ch-5 sp, ch 3, 4 dc in same sp, *3 dc in each of next 3 ch-3 sps, (5 dc, ch 1, 5 dc) in next corner ch-5 sp; rep from * twice more, 3 dc in next each of next 3 ch-3 sps, 5 dc in beg ch-5 sp, ch 1, join in 3rd ch of beg ch-3. Fasten off.

## SIDE EDGING

With RS facing and smaller hook, attach A in any corner ch-1 sp, ch 3, [sk next 2 dc, (2 dc, ch 1, 2 dc) in next st] 6 times, sk next dc, dc in corner ch-1 sp. Fasten off.

## SECOND MOTIF

Work same as Rnds 1–5 of First Motif.

## ONE-SIDE JOINING

With smaller hook, attach A to any corner ch-1 sp, ch 3, sl st in corresponding dc of edging on adjacent motif, on working motif [sk next 2 dc, 2 dc in next dc, ch 1, sl st in corresponding ch-1 sp on adjacent motif, 2 dc in same st on working motif] 6 times, sk next dc, dc in corner ch-3 sp, join in corresponding dc on adjacent motif. Fasten off.

## SIDE EDGING

With RS and side opposite joining facing, attach A with smaller hook in corner ch-1 sp, ch 3, [sk next 2 dc, (2 dc, ch 1, 2 dc) in next st] 6 times, sk next dc, dc in corner ch-1 sp. Fasten off.

## THIRD & FOURTH MOTIFS

Work same as Second Motif.

## FIFTH MOTIF

Work same as 2nd Motif through One-Side Joining. Do not work 2nd side edging.

## ROW EDGING

Holding with one long edge of row at top, with smaller hook attach A in corner ch-1 sp in upper right-hand corner, ch 3 *(counts as a dc)*, *[sk next 2 dc, (2 dc, ch 1, 2 dc) in next dc] 6 times, [(2 dc, ch 1, 2 dc) over next dc] twice, rep from * 3 times more, [sk next 2 dc, (2 dc, ch 1, 2 dc) in next dc] 6 times, sk next dc, dc in next ch-1 sp. Fasten off.

## SECOND ROW

Work same as First Row.

## ROW JOINING

Join to previous row in same manner as one-side joining.

## REMAINING ROWS

Referring to Assembly Diagram for placement, join rem motifs and rows in similar manner. **Note:** *Do not work Row Edging on Row 6.*

## BORDER

**Rnd 1:** Holding with RS facing and one long edge at top, with smaller hook, attach A in corner ch-1 sp in upper right-hand corner, ch 3 *(counts as a dc)*, dc, [ch 1, 2 dc in same sp] 3 times, *[sk next 2 dc, (2 dc, ch 1, 2 dc) in next dc] 6 times, [(2 dc, ch 1, 2 dc) over next dc] twice, rep from * 3 times more, [sk next 2 dc, (2 dc, ch 1, 2 dc) in next dc] 6 times, sk next dc, 2 dc in next corner ch-1 sp, [ch 1, 2 dc in same sp] 3 times, join in 3rd ch of beg ch-3, continue in same manner around joining in 3rd ch of beg ch-3.

**Rnd 2:** Sl st in next dc and in next ch-1 sp, ch 3, (2 dc, ch 1, 3 dc) in same sp, *(3 dc, ch 1, 3 dc) in next ch-1 sp; rep from * around, join in 3rd ch of beg ch-3.

**Rnd 3:** Sl st in next 2 dc and in next ch-1 sp, ch 3, (3 dc, ch 1, 4 dc) in same ch-1 sp, *(4 dc, ch 1, 4 dc) in next ch-1 sp; rep from * around, join in 3rd ch of beg ch-3.

Fasten off and weave in all ends. 🐾

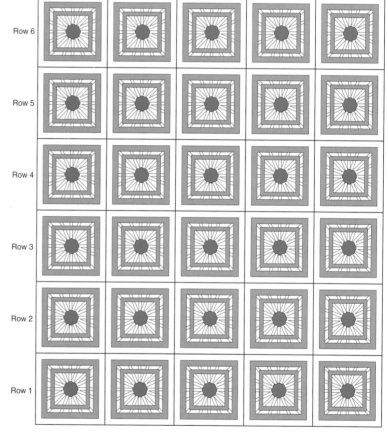

**Mystical Mist**
Assembly Diagram

# DIAGONAL DOTS

Design by Tammy Hildebrand

## FINISHED SIZE
Approximately 42 x 65 inches

## MATERIALS
- Red Heart Sport fine (sport) weight yarn (2.5 oz/ 250 yds/70g per skein): 2 skeins each #230 yellow (A), #652 limeade (B), #922 hot pink (C), #585 purple (D), and #846 skipper blue (E)
- Moda Dea Espree bulky novelty yarn (1.75 oz/90 yds/50g per skein): 3 skeins each #2117 sands (F), #2630 grassy (G), #2251 pinks (H), #2379 purples (I) and #2387 blues (J)
- Red Heart Super Saver medium (worsted) weight yarn (8 oz/452 yds/226g per skein): 3 skeins #316 soft white (K)
- Size P/15/10mm crochet hook, or size needed to obtain gauge

## GAUGE
Motif = 6 inches across
To save time, take time to check gauge.

## SPECIAL STITCHES
For **cross-stitch (cross-st):** Sk next 2 sts, dc in next st, ch 1, working over st just made, dc in first skipped st.

For **joining cross-stitch (joining cross-st):** Sk next 2 sts, dc in next st, sl st in corresponding ch-1 on adjacent motif, working over st just made, dc in first skipped st.

For **joining ch-3 sp:** Ch 1, sl st in center ch of corresponding ch-3 on adjacent motif, ch 1.

For **joining ch-1 sp:** Sl st in corresponding ch-1 on adjacent motif.

## PATTERN NOTES
Join with a slip stitch unless otherwise stated.

Motif centers are worked with 1 strand each of sport weight yarn and novelty yarn of same color held together.

## FIRST MOTIF
**Rnd 1:** With 1 strand A and 1 strand F held tog ch 4, join to form ring, ch 3 *(counts as dc)*, 15 dc in ring, join in 3rd ch of beg ch-3. *(16 dc)*

**Rnd 2:** Sl st in sp before next st, ch 3, *sk next st, (dc, ch 2, dc) in sp before next st, sk next st, dc in sp before next st; rep from * 6 times more, sk next st, (dc, ch 2, dc) in sp before next st, join in 3rd ch of beg ch-3. Fasten off.

**Rnd 3:** Attach 2 strands of K with sc in any ch-2 sp, (ch 3, sc) in same sp, **cross-st** *(see Special Stitches),* *(sc, ch 3, sc) in next ch-2 sp, cross-st over next 3 sts; rep from * 6 times more, join in first sc. Fasten off. *(8 cross-sts)*

## SECOND MOTIF
Referring to Assembly Diagram for color and placement, work same as Rnds 1 and 2 of First Motif.

**Rnd 3 (joining rnd):** Attach 2 strands of K with sc in any ch-2 sp, (**joining ch-3 sp** *{see Special Stitches},* sc) in same sp, **joining cross-st** *(see Special Stitches)* over next 3 sts, (sc, joining ch-3 sp, sc) in next ch-2 sp, cross-st over next 3 sts, [[sc, ch 3, sc) in next ch-2 sp, cross-st over next 3 sts] 6 times, join in first sc.

## REMAINING MOTIFS
Work same as for Second Motif, joining to adjacent motifs in similar manner.

## FILLER MOTIF
**Rnd 1:** Referring to Assembly Diagram for color and placement and holding 1 strand each of matching

sport and novelty yarn tog, ch 2, 8 sc in 2nd ch from hook, join in first sc. Fasten off.

**Rnd 2:** Attach 2 strands K in any st, ch 3, working in open sps between motifs, sl st in ch-1 of any cross-st, dc in same st on filler, [(dc, joining ch-3 sp, dc) in next st, [dc, **joining ch-1 sp** *(see Special Stitches)*, dc] 3 times, (dc, joining ch-3 sp, dc) in next st, join in 3rd ch of beg ch-3. Fasten off.

## BORDER

Hold with RS facing and one short end at top, attach 2 strands K with sc in center of motif joining at top right side as indicated on Assembly Diagram, *[(5 dc in next ch-1 sp, sc in next ch-3 sp) twice, 5 dc in next ch-1 sp, sc in center of motif joining] to last motif before next corner, [5 dc in next ch-1 sp, sc in next ch-3 sp] 4 times, 5 dc in next ch-1 sp, sc in center of motif joining, rep from * around, join in first sc. Fasten off. ❧

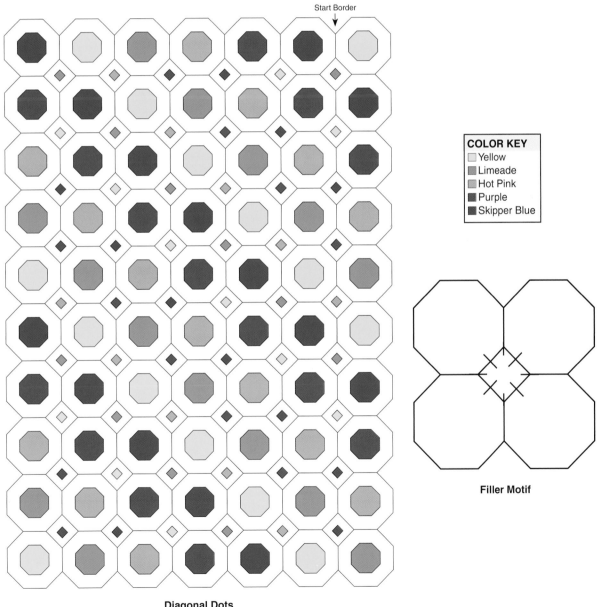

Start Border

**COLOR KEY**
▢ Yellow
▨ Limeade
▨ Hot Pink
■ Purple
■ Skipper Blue

**Filler Motif**

**Diagonal Dots**
Assembly Diagram

# DELIGHTFUL DIMENSIONS

These afghans are fun for
learning new stitch possibilities.
Who would have thought
crocheting could be so much fun?

# MEDLEY IN BLUE

Design by Darla Sims

## FINISHED SIZE

Approximately 54 x 56 inches

## MATERIALS

- Caron Simply Soft medium (worsted) weight yarn (6 oz/330 yds/170g per skein): 6 skeins #9710 country blue (A), 3 skeins #9712 soft blue (B), 2 skeins each #9709 light country blue (C) and #9736 navy (E)
- Caron Simply Soft medium (worsted) weight yarn (5 oz/260 yds/142g per skein): 2 skeins #9804 country blue ombré (D)
- Size H/8/5mm crochet hook
- Size I/9/5.5mm crochet hook or size needed to obtain gauge

## GAUGE

Motif = 7½ inches square

To save time, take time to check gauge.

## SPECIAL STITCHES

For **beginning popcorn (beg pc):** Ch 3, 4 dc in st or sp indicated, drop lp from hook, insert hook through 3rd ch of beg ch-3 and dropped lp, yo and draw through both lps on hook.

For **popcorn (pc):** 5 dc in st or sp indicated, drop lp from hook, insert hook through first dc and dropped lp, yo and draw through both lps on hook.

For **front post double crochet (fpdc):** Yo, insert hook from front to back to front around **post** (see Stitch Guide) of st indicated, pull up lp, [yo and draw through 2 lps on hook] twice.

## PATTERN NOTE

Join with a slip stitch unless otherwise stated.

## MOTIF PANELS
## Make 4.

### FIRST MOTIF

**Rnd 1:** With larger hook and E, ch 4, join to form a ring, **beg pc** (see Special Stitches) in ring, ch 2, [**pc** (see Special Stitches) in ring] 6 times, join in beg pc. Fasten off.

**Rnd 2:** Attach D in any ch-2 sp, ch 3, 2 dc in same sp, *ch 2, (pc, ch 3, pc) in next ch-2 sp (corner), ch 2**, 3 dc in next ch-2 sp; rep from * 3 times more, ending last rep at **, join in 3rd ch of beg ch-3. Fasten off.

**Rnd 3:** Attach B in ch-2 sp before any corner, ch 3, dc in same sp, *ch 2, (pc, ch 3, pc) in next corner ch-3 sp, ch 2, 2 dc in next ch-2 sp, dc in next 3 dc, 2 dc in next ch-2 sp; rep from * around, join in 3rd ch of beg ch-3. Fasten off.

**Rnd 4:** Attach A in ch-2 sp before any corner, ch 3, dc in same sp, *ch 2, (pc, ch 3, pc) in next ch-3 sp, ch 2, 2 dc in next ch-2 sp, dc in 7 dc, 2 dc in next ch-2 sp; rep from * around; join 3rd ch of beg ch-3. Fasten off.

**Rnd 5:** Attach C in ch-2 sp before any corner, ch 3, dc in same ch-2 sp, *ch 2, (pc, ch 3, pc) in next corner ch-3 sp, ch 2, 2 dc in next ch-2 sp, dc in next 11 dc, 2 dc in next ch-2 sp; rep from * around; join in 3rd ch of beg ch-3. Fasten off.

**Rnd 6:** With smaller hook attach B with sc in any corner ch-3 sp, 2 sc in same sp, *sc in next pc, 2 sc in next ch-2 sp, sc in next 15 dc, 2 sc in next ch-2 sp, sc in next pc**, 3 sc in next corner ch-3 sp; rep from * 3 times more, ending last rep as **, join in first sc. Fasten off.

### SECOND MOTIF

Work same as Rnds 1–6 of First Motif.

For **motif joining:** Hold 2 motifs with WS tog and yarn behind work, attach E with smaller hook, pull

yarn from WS to RS through corresponding corner sc of both motifs, insert hook in **back lp** of motif away from you, insert hook in **back lp** corresponding lp on motif closest to you *(back lps of both pieces are now overlapping),* yo and pull yarn through both lps on hook, ch 1, *insert hook in next **back lp** of motif away from you, insert hook in corresponding **back lp** of motif closest to you, pull yarn through from underneath and through both lps; rep from * across. Fasten off.

## REMAINING MOTIFS
Work as for Second Motif, joining to previous motif to form 4 panels with 7 motifs in each panel.

## CABLE PANELS
**Make 5.**
**Row 1:** With larger hook and A, ch 12, sc in 2nd ch from hook and in each rem ch. Turn. *(11 sc)*
**Row 2 & all even-numbered rows:** Ch 1, sc in each sc. Turn.
**Row 3:** Ch 1, sc in first 5 sc, pc around post *(see Stitch Guide)* of next st on row before last, sk next sc on working row, sc in next 5 sc. Turn.
**Row 5:** Ch 1, sc in first 3 sc, 2 fpdc around post of next sc on row before last, on working row sk next 2 sts, sc in next sc, sk next pc and next sc on row before last, 2 fpdc around post of next sc, sk next 2 sc on working row, sc in next 3 sc. Turn.
**Rows 7, 9 & 11:** Ch 1, sc in first 3 sc, fpdc around each of next 2 fpdc, sk next 2 sc on working row, sc in next sc, fpdc around each of next 2 fpdc, sk next 2 sc on working row, sc in next 3 sc. Turn.
**Row 13:** Ch 1, sc in next 5 sc, keeping last lp of each fpdc on hook, fpdc around each of 4 fpdc on row before last, yo and draw through all 5 lps on hook *(cl),* sk next sc on working row, sc in next 5 sc. Turn.
**Row 15:** Ch 1, sc in next 5 sts, pc around post of cl on row before last, sk next sc on working row, sc in next 5 sts. Turn.
**Row 16:** Ch 1, sc in each sc. Turn.
[Rep Rows 5–16] 16 times more. Fasten off.

## EDGING
Hold with RS facing and 1 short end at top, with smaller hook, attach B with sc in upper right-hand corner, 2 sc in same sp, sc in each st across last row of panel to next corner, 3 sc next st, working along side to next corner, sc in ends of rows keeping piece flat, 3 sc in next st, working in unused lps of beg ch, sc in each lp to next corner, 3 sc in next st, working along side to next corner, sc in ends of rows keeping piece flat and have same number of sc as on opposite long edge, join in first sc. Fasten off.

## PANEL JOINING
Referring to Assembly Diagram for placement, join motif panels to cable panels in same manner as for motif joinings.

## BORDER
**Rnd 1:** With smaller hook attach A with an sc in 2nd sc of upper right-hand corner, sc in each sc working 3 sc in each outer corner, join in first sc.
**Rnd 2:** Ch 3, dc in each sc, working 3 dc in 2nd sc of each 3-sc corner; join in 3rd ch of beg ch-3.
**Rnd 3:** Attach E in 2nd dc of any 3-dc corner, beg pc in same sp, *dc in next 3 dc, [pc in next dc, dc in next 5 dc]; rep between [ ] to next corner and adjusting as necessary to end last rep with dc in next 3 dc, pc in next corner; rep from * around, join in beg pc. Fasten off and weave in all ends. ❧

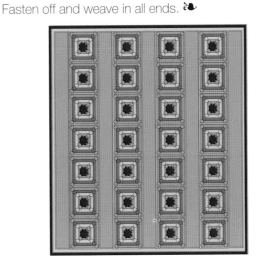

**Medley in Blue**
Assembly Diagram

# GRACIOUS GARDEN

Design by Darla Sims

## FINISHED SIZE
Approximately 44 x 56 inches

## MATERIALS
- Red Heart Classic medium (worsted) weight yarn (3.5 oz/198 yds/100g per skein): 6 skeins each #719 lily pink (A) and #622 pale sage green (B), 5 skeins #1 white (C), 3 skeins #730 grenadine (D)
- Size H/8/5mm crochet hook or size needed to obtain gauge

## GAUGE
8 sc = 2 inches
To save time, take time to check gauge.

## SPECIAL STITCHES
For **leaf stitch (leaf st):** [Yo twice, insert hook in st indicated, yo, draw through 2 lps on hook] 3 times, yo and draw through all 4 lps on hook.

For **beginning popcorn (beg pc):** Ch 3, 4 dc around **post** (see Stitch Guide) of st indicated, drop lp from hook, insert hook through 3rd ch of beg ch-3 and dropped lp, yo and draw through both lps on hook.

For **popcorn (pc):** 5 dc around **post** (see Stitch Guide) of st indicated, drop lp from hook, insert hook through first dc and dropped lp, yo and draw through both lps on hook.

## PATTERN NOTE
Join with a slip stitch unless otherwise stated.

## FIRST PANEL
**Rnd 1:** With C, ch 144, sc in 2nd ch from hook and in each ch to last ch, 3 sc in next ch, working along opposite side in unused lps of beg ch, sc to first sc,

2 sc in same ch, join in first sc. Fasten off.

**Rnd 2:** Attach B in center sc at one end of panel, ch 6 (counts as tr and ch-2 sp), **leaf st** (see Special Stitches) in same st, sk next 2 sc, [(leaf st, ch 2, tr, ch 2, leaf st) in next st (leaf group), sk next 5 sc] 23 times, leaf group in next st, sk next 2 sc, leaf group in next st, sk next 2 sc, [leaf group, sk next 5 sc] 23 times, sk next 2 sc, leaf in same sp as beg ch-6, ch 2, join in 4th ch of beg ch-6.

**Rnd 3:** Ch 6 (counts as dc and ch 3 sp), *dc in sp between leaf groups, ch 3 **, 3 dc in next tr; rep from * around ending at **, 2 dc in same st as beg ch, join in 3rd dc of beg ch-6. Fasten off.

**Rnd 4:** Attach D around post of center dc at 1 end of panel, **beg pc** (see Special Stitches) around same dc, ch 5, **pc** (see Special Stitches) around post of next dc, *ch 3, pc around post of 2nd dc of next 3-dc group, ch 3, pc around post of next dc; rep from * to 3-dc group at end of panel, ch 5, pc around post of 2nd dc of 3-dc group at end of panel, ch 5, pc around post of next dc, [ch 3, pc around post of 2nd dc of next 3-dc group, ch 3, pc around post of next dc] rep between [ ] to beg pc, ch 5, join in beg pc. Change to C by drawing lp through. Fasten off D.

**Rnd 5:** Working over chs of Rnds 3 and 4, 7 dc in next ch-5 sp, sc in top of next pc (insert hook through top of pc and dc behind it), *5 dc in next ch-3 sp, insert hook into top of next pc; with A (do not cut C) and pull through, sl st around post of dc to left of pc, [ch 6, sl st around same post] 5 times, ch 6, [sl st around dc to right of same pc, ch 5] 6 times, sl st to beg sl st drawing C through (flower made), with C, 5 dc in next ch-3 sp, sc through top of next pc and dc behind it**, rep from * to next ch-5 sp, 7 dc in ch-5 sp, flower around dc next pc, 7 dc in next ch-5 sp,

Continued on page 92

# ZIGZAG SQUARES

Design by Bonnie Pierce

### FINISHED SIZE

Approximately 37 x 50 inches

### MATERIALS

- Red Heart Super Saver medium (worsted) weight yarn (8 oz/452 yds/226g per skein): 3 skeins #376 burgundy (A), 2 skeins each #400 grey heather (B) and #311 white (C), 1 skein #313 aran (D)
- Size H/8/5mm crochet hook or size needed to obtain gauge

### GAUGE

Motif = 7½ inches square

To save time, take time to check gauge.

### SPECIAL STITCH

For **front post double crochet (fpdc):** Yo, insert hook from front to back to front around **post** (see Stitch Guide) of st indicated, pull up lp, [yo and draw through 2 lps on hook] twice.

### PATTERN NOTE

Join with a slip stitch unless otherwise stated.

### FIRST MOTIF

**Rnd 1:** With D make a loose slip knot on hook, ch 3 (counts as dc), 19 dc in beg lp, join in 3rd ch of beg ch-3. Fasten off. Tighten beg lp. (20 dc)

**Rnd 2:** Attach B from front to back to front around **post** (see Stitch Guide) of any dc, ch 5 (counts as dc and ch-2 sp), [**fpdc** (see Special Stitches), ch 2] twice around same dc, fpdc around same dc,*sk next dc, [fpdc around post of next dc] twice, sk next dc, [fpdc, ch 2] 3 times around post of next dc, fpdc around post of same dc, rep from * twice more, sk next dc, [fpdc around post of next dc] twice, sk next dc, join in 3rd ch of beg ch-5. Fasten off.

**Rnd 3:** Attach C in corner ch-2 sp, ch 5 (counts as dc and ch-2 sp), dc in same sp, ch 1, *[dc in next dc, ch 1] 6 times, (dc, ch 2, dc) in next st (corner); rep from * twice more, ch 1, [dc in next dc, ch 1] 6 times, join in 3rd ch of beg ch 5. Drop C, do not fasten off.

**Rnd 4:** Attach A around post of first dc of any corner, ch 2 (counts as hdc), hdc around post of same dc, 2 hdc in next ch-2 sp, 2 hdc around post of next dc, working in front of Rnd 3, 2 hdc in corner ch-2 sp of Rnd 2 (after corner), *[2 hdc around post of next dc (inserting hook from left to right), 2 hdc over next ch-1 sp, 2 hdc over post of next dc (inserting hook from right to left), working in front of Rnd 3, 2 hdc in same dc of Rnd 2 as next dc] twice, 2 hdc around post of next dc (inserting hook from left to right), 2 hdc over next ch-1 sp, 2 hdc over post of next dc (inserting hook from right to left), working in front of Rnd 3, 2 hdc in corner ch-2 sp of Rnd 2 (before corner), 2 hdc around post of next dc, 2 hdc over next ch-2 sp, 2 hdc over post of next dc, working in front of Rnd 3, 2 hdc in ch-2 sp of Rnd 2 (after corner); rep from * 3 times more, join 2nd ch of beg ch-2. Fasten off. (16 zigzags)

**Rnd 5:** With C, ch 6 (counts as dc and ch 3), working in unused ch-1 sps of Rnd 3, *4 dc in each of next 4 ch-1 sps, ch 3 (corner); rep from * twice more, 4 dc in each of next 3 ch-1 sps, 3 dc in next ch-1 sp, join in 3rd ch of beg ch-5. Fasten off.

**Rnd 6:** Attach D with sc in any corner ch-3 sp, (sc, ch 1, 2 sc) in same sp, sc in next 16 sts, *(2 sc, ch 1, 2 sc) in next corner ch-3 sp, sc in next 16 sts; rep from * twice more. Fasten off.

**Rnd 7:** Attach B with sc in any corner ch-1 sp, 2 sc in same sp, sc in next 20 sc, *3 sc in next corner ch-1 sp, sc in next 20 sc; rep from * twice more, join in first sc. Fasten off.

**Rnd 8:** Attach A with sc in 2nd sc of any 3-sc corner, 2 sc in same corner, sc in next 22 sc *3 sc in next corner sc, sc in next 22 sc; rep from * twice more, join in first sc. Fasten off.

## SECOND & THIRD MOTIFS

Work same as First Motif.

To **join motifs:** Referring to Assembly Diagram for placement hold First and Second Motifs with WS tog, join with sc in corresponding corner sc of both motifs, working through sts of both motifs at same time, sc in each sc to next corner sc, sc in corresponding corner sc of Third Motif, working through sts of First and Third Motifs at same time sc across. Fasten off.

## REMAINING MOTIFS

Referring to Assembly Diagram for placement, make additional motifs and join diagonally in similar manner making sure all 4-corner joinings are secure.

## BORDER

**Rnd 1:** Holding with RS facing and one short edge at top, join A with sc in upper right-hand corner sc, 2 sc in same sp, *sc in each sc to 2nd sc of next 3-sc corner, 3 sc in corner sc; rep from * twice more; sc in each sc to beg corner, join in first sc.

**Rnd 2:** Sc in each sc working 3 sc in 2nd sc of each 3-sc corner.
Fasten off and weave in all ends. 🦋

| | | | | |
|---|---|---|---|---|
| 35 | 33 | 30 | 26 | 21 |
| 34 | 31 | 27 | 22 | 16 |
| 32 | 28 | 23 | 17 | 11 |
| 29 | 24 | 18 | 12 | 7 |
| 25 | 19 | 13 | 8 | 4 |
| 20 | 14 | 9 | 5 | 2 |
| 15 | 10 | 6 | 3 | 1 |

**Zigzag Squares**
Assembly Diagram

# GRACIOUS GARDEN Continued from page 88

sc in top of next pc, rep from * to ** to next ch-5 sp, 7 dc in next ch-5 sp, flower around beg pc, join in first dc. Fasten off. *(50 flowers: 24 along each side, 1 at each end)*

## SECOND THROUGH SEVENTH PANELS

Work as for First Panel, until first half of Rnd 5 is complete, ending with flower at end of panel, 7 dc in next ch-5 sp, *sc in top of next pc, 2 dc in next ch-4 sp, sl st in center dc of corresponding dc on adjacent panel, 3 dc in same ch-4 sp on working panel, flower around pc, 2 dc in next ch-5 sp, sl st in center dc of corresponding dc on adjacent panel, 3 dc in same ch-4 sp on working panel; rep from * to end of panel, working 7 dc in last ch-5 sp, flower around end pc, join in first dc.

Fasten off and weave in all ends. 🦋

# ROLL STITCH RHAPSODY

Design by Bonnie Pierce

## FINISHED SIZE

Approximately 35 x 51 inches

## MATERIALS

- Red Heart Super Saver medium (worsted) weigh yarn (8 oz/452 yds/226g per skein): 2 skeins #311 white (A), 2 skeins each #347 light periwinkle (B) and #531 light plum (C)
- Size H/8/5mm crochet hook or size needed to obtain gauge

## GAUGE

Motif = 9 inches square
To save time, take time to check gauge.

## SPECIAL STITCHES

For **picot:** Ch 3, sl st in 3rd ch from hook.

For **10-roll stitch (10-roll st):** Yo 10 times *loosely and evenly*, insert hook into next st, yo, draw up a lp even with the 10 lps, yo, draw through all 12 lps (wiggling the hook and rolling the yarn back and forth).

For **15-roll stitch (15-roll st):** Yo 15 times *loosely and evenly*, insert hook into next st, yo, draw up a lp even with the 15 lps, yo, draw through all 17 lps (wiggling the hook and rolling the yarn back and forth).

## PATTERN NOTE

Join with a slip stitch unless otherwise stated.

## FIRST MOTIF

**Rnd 1:** With A make loose slip knot on hook, ch 3 *(counts as dc),* 15 dc in beg lp, join in 3rd ch of beg ch-3. Fasten off. Tighten beg lp. *(16 dc)*

**Rnd 2:** Attach B in any dc, ch 3, dc in same st, ch 2, 2 dc in next st *(corner),* *ch 3, **picot** *(see Special Stitches),* ch 1, sl st in next 2 sts, ch 5, picot in 3rd ch from hook**, (2 dc, ch 2, 2 dc) in next st *(corner),* rep from * 3 times more, ending at **, join 3rd ch of beg ch-3. Fasten off.

**Rnd 3:** Attach C in any corner ch-2 sp, ch 3 (2 dc, ch 2, 3 dc) in same sp, dc in next 4 dc, *(3 dc, ch 2, 3 dc) in corner ch-2 sp, dc in next 4 dc, rep from * twice more. Fasten off.

**Rnd 4:** Attach A in any corner ch-2 sp, ch 3, *(**10-roll st,** *{see Special Stitches}* ch 1, 10-roll st, ch 2, 10 roll-st, ch 1, 10-roll st, ch 1) in same sp, dc in next 10 dc, ch 1; rep from * 3 times more; join in 3rd ch of beg ch-3. Fasten off.

**Rnd 5:** Attach B with sc in any corner ch-2 sp, 2 sc in same sp, *sc in next 2 ch-1 sps and in next 4 dc, [yo 3 times, insert hook in next picot on Rnd 2 and draw up lp, (yo and draw through 2 lps on hook) 3 times, insert hook in next st on working rnd, draw up lp, yo and draw through all 3 lps on hook], rep between [ ] once, sc in next 4 dc and in next 2 ch-1 sps**, 3 sc in next corner ch-2 sp, rep from * 3 times more, ending last rep at **, join in first sc. Fasten off.

**Rnd 6:** Attach C with sc in 2nd sc of any 3-sc corner, 2 sc in same sc, *sc in next 7 sts, sl st in next st, ch 2, **15-roll st** *(see Special Stitches)* in same st, sl st in next st, sc in next 7 sts**, 3 sc in next st; rep * 3 times more, ending last rep at **, join in first sc. Fasten off.

**Rnd 7:** Attach A in 2nd sc of any 3-sc corner, ch 3 (dc, ch 2, 2 dc) in same sc, *[ch 1, sk next st, dc in next st] 4 times, ch 1, dc in next ch-2 sp, ch 1, dc in

next st, [ch 1, sk next st, dc in next st] 3 times, ch 1**, (2 dc, ch 2, 2 dc) in 2nd sc of 3-sc corner; rep from * 3 times more, ending last rep at **, join in 3rd ch of beg ch-3.

**Rnd 8:** Sl st in next dc and in next ch-2 sp, ch 3, dc in same sp, *ch 1, sk next dc, dc in next dc, [ch 1, dc in next ch-1 sp] 10 times, ch 1, sk next dc, dc in next dc, ch 1**, (2 dc, ch 2, 2 dc) in next corner ch-2 sp; rep from * 3 times more, ending last rep at **, 2 dc in beg corner, join with hdc in 3rd ch of beg ch-3. Fasten off.

## SECOND MOTIF

Work same as First Motif, **do not fasten off** at end of rnd 8.

To **join motifs:** Sl st in corresponding corner of adjacent motif, holding RS tog and working through sts of both motifs at same time, sc in each st and sp across one side.

## REMAINING MOTIFS

Referring to Assembly Diagram for placement, continue to join motifs in this manner until 4 motifs are joined.

Join additional rows in same manner, then join rows in same manner, being sure all 4-corner joinings are secure.

## BORDER

**Rnd 1:** Hold with RS facing and one short edge at top, join in upper right-hand corner, ch 3, dc in same sp, ch 1, *[sk next dc, dc in next dc, {ch 1, dc in next ch-1 sp} 13 times, ch 1, sk next dc, dc in next dc, ch 1, {dc in corner of next motif, ch 1} twice]; rep between [ ] to next corner, sk next dc, dc in next dc, [ch 1, dc in next ch-1 sp] 13 times, ch 1, sk next dc, dc in next dc, ch 1**, (2 dc, ch 2, 2 dc) in corner ch-2 sp, rep from * 3 times more, ending last rep at **, 2 dc in first corner, join with hdc in 3rd ch of beg ch-3.

**Rnd 2:** Sl st in sp formed by joining hdc, ch 3, dc in same sp, *sk next dc, dc in next dc, [ch 1, dc in next ch-1 sp], rep between [ ] to next corner, sk next dc, dc in next dc**, (2 dc, ch 2, 2 dc) in corner ch-2 sp; rep from * 3 times more, ending last rep at **, 2 dc in first corner, join with hdc in 3rd ch of beg ch-3.

**Rnd 3:** Sl st in sp formed by joining hdc, ch 6, picot in 3rd ch from hook, dc in same sp, picot, *2 dc, picot, sk next dc, dc in next dc, [ch 1, dc in next ch-1 sp, picot, dc in next ch-1 sp], rep between [ ] to next corner, sk next dc, dc in next dc, picot**, [dc, picot, dc, picot, 2 dc, picot] in corner ch-2 sp; rep from * 3 times more, ending last rep at **, join in 3rd ch of beg ch-3.

Fasten off and weave in all ends. 🦋

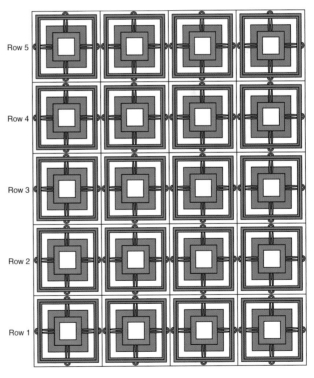

**Roll Stitch Rhapsody**
Assembly Diagram

# DIAMOND BOUCLÉ

Design by Joyce Nordstrom

## FINISHED SIZE
Approximately 52 x 68 inches

## MATERIALS
- TLC Amore medium (worsted) weight yarn (6 oz/ 290 yds/170g per skein): 3 skeins #3103 vanilla (A), 2 skeins each #3710 rose (B), #3627 light thyme (C) and #3005 sand (D)
- Size I/9/5.5mm crochet hook or size needed to obtain gauge

## GAUGE
Motif = 3½ inches wide x 5 inches long
To save time, take time to check gauge.

## SPECIAL STITCH
For **decrease (dec):** [Yo, pull up lp in next ch-1 sp, yo and draw through 2 lps on hook] twice, yo and draw through all 3 lps on hook.

## PATTERN NOTES
Join with a slip stitch unless otherwise stated.
Round 1 of motif is WS.

## FIRST ROW
### FIRST MOTIF
**Rnd 1 (WS):** With B ch 5, join to form a ring, sl st ring, ch 1, *2 sc, hdc, dc, tr, ch 2 (end sp), tr, dc, hdc, 2 sc in ring; rep from * once more, join in first sc.

**Rnd 2:** Ch 3 (counts as hdc and ch-1 sp); *[sk next st, hdc in next st, ch 1] twice; (dc, ch 1, dc) in next ch-2 end sp, ch 1, [hdc in next st, ch 1, sk next st] twice**, (hdc in next sc, ch 1) twice; rep from * once more, ending at **, hdc in next sc, ch 1, join in 2nd ch of beg ch 3. Turn. (16 ch-1 sps)

**Rnd 3 (RS):** Sl st in next ch-1 sp, ch 3, hdc in same sp, *(2 hdc in next ch-1 sp) 3 times, (2 dc, ch 2, 2 dc) next ch-1 end sp; (2 hdc in next sp) 3 times**, (hdc, ch 1, hdc) in next ch-1 sp (side sp); rep from * once more, ending at **, join in 2nd ch of beg ch-3. Fasten off.

**Rnd 4:** With RS facing, attach A in either ch-2 end sp, ch 4 (counts as dc and ch-1 sp), working in **back lps** only, *[sc in next st, ch 1, sk next st] 4 times, sc in next st, (hdc, ch 2, hdc) in side ch-1 sp, working in **back lps** only, sc in next st, [ch 1, sk next st, sc in next st] 4 times**; (dc, ch 3, dc) in ch-2 end sp; rep from * once more, ending at **; (dc, ch 3) in beg end sp, join in 3rd ch of ch 4. Fasten off.

## SECOND ROW
### FIRST MOTIF
Work same as Rnds 1–3 of First Motif of First Row.

**Rnd 4 (joining rnd):** With RS facing, attach A in either ch-2 end sp, ch 4 (counts as dc and ch-1 sp), *working in **back lps** only, [sc in next st, ch 1, sk next st] 4 times, sc in next st, (hdc, ch 2, hdc) in side ch-1 sp, working in **back lps** only, sc in next st, [ch 1, sk next st, sc in next st] 4 times**; dc in ch-2 end sp, ch 1, sl st in corresponding end sp on previous motif, dc in same end sp on working motif; rep from * to **; (dc, ch 3) in beg end sp, join in 3rd ch of ch 4. Fasten off.

### SECOND MOTIF
Referring to Assembly Diagram for color and placement, work same as Rnds 1–3 of First Motif of First Row.

**Rnd 4 (joining rnd):** With RS facing, attach A, in either end sp, ch 4 (counts as dc and ch-1 sp), sl st in corresponding side sp of adjacent motif; [working in **back lps** only of working motif, sc in next st, ch 1, sk next st, sl st in corresponding ch-1 sp of adjacent motif]; rep between [ ] 3 times more, hdc in side sp of working motif, ch 1, sl st in joined end sps of adjacent motifs, hdc in same sp on working motif, rep between [ ] 4 times, dc in end sp, ch 1, sl st in corresponding end sp on adjacent motif, dc in same sp on working motif, working in **back lps** only, [sc in next st, ch 1, sk next st] 4 times, sc in next st, (hdc, ch 2, hdc) in side ch-1 sp, working in **back lps** only, sc in next st, [ch 1, sk next st, sc in next st] 4 times; (dc, ch 3) in beg end sp, join in 3rd ch of ch 4. Fasten off.

## REMAINING MOTIFS

Referring to Assembly Diagram for color and placement, work same as Second Motif, joining to adjacent motifs in similar manner and making sure all 4-corner joinings are secure.

## BORDER

**Rnd 1:** With RS facing, attach A with sc in end ch-3 sp of motif in upper right-hand corner ch 3, (ch 3, sc) in same sp, *[sc in next ch-1 sp, ch 1] 6 times, sk side sp of same motif, sc in joining, sk side sp of next motif, [sc in next ch-1 sp, ch 1] 6 times; (hdc, ch 3, hdc) in end sp of same motif; rep from * 8 times more, [sc in next ch-1 sp, ch 1] 6 times, (sc, ch 2, sc) in next side sp, **[sc in next ch-1 sp, ch 1] 6 times, sk end sp of same motif, sc in joining, sk end sp of next motif, [sc in next ch-1 sp, ch 1] 6 times, (sc, ch 2, sc) in next side sp; rep from ** 7 times, [sc in next ch-1 sp, ch 1] 6 times,  (hdc, ch 3, hdc) in end sp of same motif, *[sc in next ch-1 sp, ch 1] 6 times, sk side sp of same motif, sc in joining, sk side sp of next motif, [sc in next ch-1 sp, ch 1] 6 times; (hdc, ch 3, hdc) in end sp of same motif; rep from * 8 times more, [sc in next ch-1 sp, ch 1] 6 times, (sc, ch 2, sc) in next side sp, **[sc in next ch-1 sp, ch 1]

6 times, sk end sp of same motif, sc in joining, sk end sp of next motif, [sc in next ch-1 sp, ch 1] 6 times, (sc, ch 2, sc) in next side sp; rep from ** 7 times, [sc in next ch-1 sp, ch 1] 6 times, join in 2nd ch of beg ch-3. Turn.

**Rnd 2:** Sl st in next ch-1 sp, ch 3, dc in same sp, work 2 dc in each ch-1 sp, 5 dc in each outside end sp and a **dec** *(see Special Stitch)* at each inside corner, join in 3rd ch of beg ch-3. Fasten off.

**Rnd 3:** Attach B in **back lp** of any dc, working in **back lps** only, [sl st in next dc, ch 1, sk next st] around. Fasten off and weave in all ends. ❧

**COLOR KEY**
■ Rose
■ Thyme
■ Sand

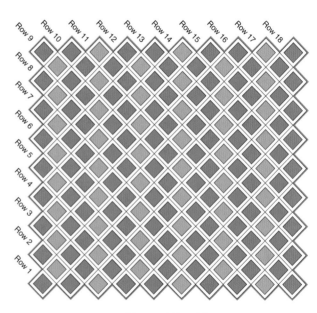

**Diamond Bouclé**
Assembly Diagram

# BERRIES & CREAM

Design by Bonnie Pierce

## FINISHED SIZE
Approximately 35 x 55 inches

## MATERIALS
- Red Heart Classic medium (worsted) weight yarn (3.5 oz/198 yds/100g per skein): 6 skeins #882 country blue (A)
- Red Heart Super Saver medium (worsted) weight yarn (8 oz/452 yds/226g per skein): 1 skein each #316 soft white (B), #372 rose pink (C), #378 claret (D), #376 burgundy (E) and #374 country rose (F)
- Size G/6/4mm crochet hook or size needed to obtain gauge
- Size H/8/5mm crochet hook or size needed to obtain gauge

## GAUGE
Motif = 5½ inches square
To save time, take time to check gauge.

## SPECIAL STITCH
For **berry stitch (berry st):** (Sc, hdc, 3 dc, hdc) in st indicated, turn; sk first 5 sts, sl st in next sc; turn.

## PATTERN NOTE
Join with a slip stitch unless otherwise stated.

## FIRST MOTIF
**Rnd 1:** With smaller hook and B, make slip knot on hook, ch 1, 8 sc in beg lp, join in first sc, tighten beg lp.

**Rnd 2:** Ch 5 *(counts as dc and ch-2 sp),* [dc in next st, ch 2] 7 times, join in 3rd ch of beg ch-5. Fasten off.

**Rnd 3 (berry rnd):** Attach C in any dc, ch 1, **berry st** *(see Special Stitch)* in same dc, [ch 3, berry st in next dc] 7 times, join in first sc. Fasten off. *(8 berry sts)*

**Rnd 4:** Attach B in any ch-2 sp of Rnd 2, ch 6 *(counts as tr and ch-2 sp),* sc in the **back lp** of last hdc of next berry st, ch 2, *tr in next ch-2 sp, ch 2, sc in **back lp** of last hdc of next berry st, ch 2; rep from * 6 times more, sl st in 4th ch of beg ch-6.

**Rnd 5:** Ch 6, sl st in same st, *ch 2, dc in next sc, ch 2, (sl st, ch 6, sl st) in next tr; rep from * 6 times more, ch 2, dc in next sc, ch 2, join in beg sl st.

**Rnd 6:** Sl st in next ch-6 sp, ch 1, 12 sc in same sp, *ch 2, dc in next dc, ch 2, 12 sc in next ch-6 sp, sc in next dc**; 12 sc in next ch-6 sp; rep from * 3 times more, ending last rep at **, join in first sc.

**Rnd 7:** With larger hook, attach A in any dc, ch 5, *(counts as dc and ch-2 sp),* (dc, ch 2, dc, ch 2, dc) in same sc *(corner),* *[sl st in back horizontal bar of 3rd sc of next 12-sc group, ch 4, sl st in back horizontal bar of 9th sc of same 12-sc group], ch 2, rep between [ ] once**; [dc in next dc, ch 2] 3 times, dc in same dc *(corner);* rep from * 3 times more, ending last rep at **, join 3rd ch of beg ch-5.

**Rnd 8:** Ch 3 *(counts as a dc),* *dc in next ch-2 sp and in next dc, (2 dc, ch 1, 2 dc) in next ch-2 sp *(corner),* dc in next dc, in next ch-2 sp, in next dc and in next sl st; 3 hdc in next ch-4 sp, 2 hdc in next ch-2 sp, 3 hdc in next ch-4 sp, dc in sl st **, dc in next dc; rep from * 3 times more, ending last rep at **, join in 3rd ch of beg ch-3.

**Rnd 9:** With smaller hook, sc in each st working 3 sc in each corner ch-1 sp, join in first sc. Fasten off.

## SECOND MOTIF
Referring to Assembly Diagram for berry color and motif placement, work same as Rnds 1–9 of First Motif.

To **join motifs**: Hold 2 motifs with RS tog, join in corresponding corner ch-1 sps, ch 1, sc in same

sp, sc in **back lps** of corresponding sts across to next corner ch-1 sp, sc in corresponding corner sps. Fasten off.

## REMAINING MOTIFS

Referring to Assembly Diagram for color and placement, work rem motifs as for Second Motif, joining rows in similar manner and making sure all 4-corner joinings are secure.

## BORDER

**Rnd 1:** Hold with RS facing, join with sc in **back lp** of corner st in upper right-hand corner, working in **back lps** only, sc in each st around, join in first sc.

**Rnd 2:** Ch 1, working in both lps, sc in each st working 3 sc in each corner, join in first sc.

**Rnd 3:** Ch 1, working from left to right, reverse sc in each st around; join in first sc.

Fasten off and weave in all ends.

## FINISHING

Using medium iron, block lightly and briefly with a warm damp pressing cloth on the WS of the afghan. ❧

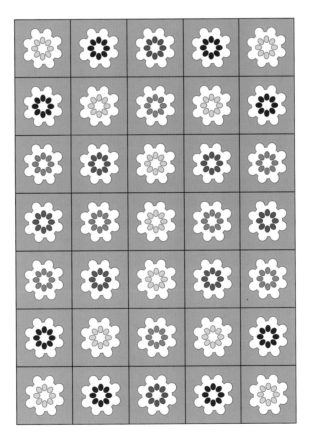

**COLOR KEY**
- ☐ Rose Pink
- ■ Claret
- ■ Burgundy
- ▦ County Rose

**Berries & Cream**
Assembly Diagram

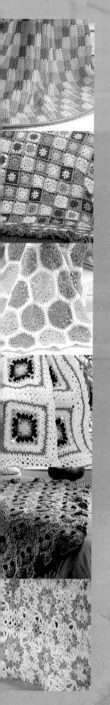

# CHILD'S PLAY

Bring a smile to a child's face with an afghan they can rely on to comfort them at bedtime or during other stresses of life.

SKILL LEVEL
INTERMEDIATE

YARN WEIGHT
4 MEDIUM

# STAIR STEPS

Design by Ann E. Smith

## FINISHED SIZE
Approximately 36 x 41 inches

## MATERIALS
- Red Heart Kids worsted weight yarn (5 oz/302 yds/140g per skein): 2 skeins each of #2390 red (A), #2230 yellow (B) and #2252 orange (C)
- Size H/8/5mm crochet hook or size needed to obtain gauge

## GAUGE
Motif = 1½ inches square
To save time, take time to check gauge.

## PATTERN NOTE
Afghan is made diagonally from corner to corner.

## FIRST MOTIF
**Row 1 (RS):** With A, ch 6, sc in 2nd ch from hook and in each ch across. Turn. *(5 sts)*
**Row 2:** Ch 1, sc in each sc across. Turn.
**Rows 3–5:** Rep Row 2. Fasten off.

## FIRST DIAGONAL ROW
### FIRST MOTIF
**Row 1 (RS):** With B, ch 6, sc in 2nd ch from hook and in each ch across, sl st in edge st along right edge of Rows 1 and 2 of First Motif. Turn.
**Row 2:** Ch 1, sk first 2 sl sts, sc in next 5 sc. Turn.
**Row 3:** Ch 1, sc in first 5 sc, sl st in edge sts along right edge of next 2 rows of First Motif. Turn.
**Row 4:** Rep Row 2.
**Row 5:** Ch 1, sc in first 5 sc, sl st in first sc on Row 5 of First Motif.

## SECOND MOTIF
**Row 1 (RS):** Ch 1, sc in same sc and in next 4 sc. Turn.
**Row 2:** Ch 1, sc in each sc across. Turn.
**Rows 3–5:** Rep Row 2. Fasten off.

## SECOND DIAGONAL ROW
### FIRST MOTIF
**Row 1 (RS):** With C, ch 6, sc in 2nd ch from hook and in each ch across, sl st in edge sc along right edge of Rows 1 and 2 of first motif of adjacent diagonal row. Turn.
**Row 2:** Ch 1, sk first 2 sl sts, sc in next 5 sc. Turn.
**Row 3:** Ch 1, sc in first 5 sc, sl st in edge sts along right edge of next 2 rows of adjacent motif. Turn.
**Row 4:** Rep Row 2.
**Row 5:** Ch 1, sc in first 5 sc, sl st in first sc on Row 5 of adjacent motif.

### SECOND MOTIF
**Row 1 (RS):** Ch 1, sc in same sc and in next 4 sc, sl st in edge st of next 2 rows on adjacent motif. Turn.
**Row 2:** Ch 1, sk first 2 sl sts, sc in next 5 sc. Turn.
**Row 3:** Ch 1, sc in first 5 sc, sl st in edge sts of next 2 rows of adjacent motif. Turn.
**Row 4:** Rep Row 2.
**Row 5:** Ch 1, sc in first 5 sc, sl st in first sc of Row 5 of adjacent motif.

### THIRD MOTIF
**Row 1 (RS):** Ch 1, sc in same sc and in next 4 sc. Turn.
**Row 2:** Ch 1, sc in each sc across. Turn.
**Rows 3–5:** Rep Row 2. Fasten off.

## REMAINING DIAGONAL ROWS
### FIRST HALF
Referring to Assembly Diagram for color and placement, continue to alternate A, B and C in stair-step fashion until diagonal Row 24 has been completed. *The afghan now looks like a misshapen triangle.*

### SECOND HALF
With RS facing, attach B in first sc of motif indicated on Assembly Diagram, ch 1, sc in same sc and in next 4 sc, sl st in corresponding rows on adjacent motif. Add B motif on top of each A motif, ending by joining last B motif to right side of last A motif. Referring to Assembly Diagram for color and placement, continue adding motifs in this manner, until the afghan is shaped as a rectangle and there are 4 red corners.

## BORDER
**Rnd 1 (RS):** With RS facing, attach A in upper right-hand corner sc, ch 1, 3 sc in same sc and in next 4 A sc, continue around working 5 sc across each block to corner block, sc in next 4 sc, 3 sc in next sc *(corner)*, sc in next 4 rows, sc in next 5 rows of next block, continue in same manner to first sc; join in first sc. Fasten off. *(125 sc along each side + 1 sc in each corner)*

**Rnd 2:** Attach C in 2nd sc of any 3-sc corner, ch 1, 3 sc in same sc, sc in next 5 sc, changing to B in last sc, continue around alternating 5 B sc and 5 C sc, ending with 5 C sc before corner and working 3 C sc in 2nd sc of each 3- sc corner, join in first sc. Fasten off.

**Rnd 3:** Attach A in **back lp** of any sc, working in **back lps** only, sc in each sc around, working 3 sc in each corner, join in first sc.

**Rnd 4:** Sl st in each sc around, join in first sl st. Fasten off and weave in all ends.

**COLOR KEY**
A Red
B Yellow
C Orange

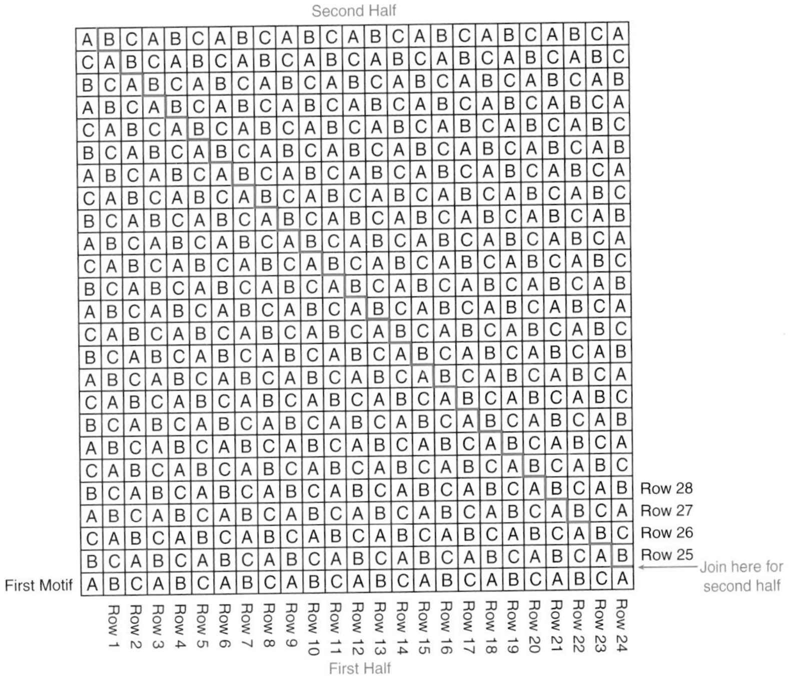

**Stair Steps**
Assembly Diagram

# PLAYFUL COLORS

Design by Darla Sims

## FINISHED SIZE

Approximately 33 x 36 inches

## MATERIALS

- Lion Brand Microspun (2.5 oz/168 yds/70g per skein): 6 skeins #148 turquoise (A); 1 skein each #147 purple (B), #143 lavender (C), #194 lime (D), #103 coral (E), #113 cherry red (F), #158 buttercup (G) and #186 mango (H)
- Size G/6/4mm crochet hook
- Size H/8/5mm crochet hook or size needed to obtain gauge

**COLOR KEY**
A Turquoise
B Purple
C Lavender
D Lime
E Coral
F Red
G Buttercup
H Mango

## GAUGE

Motif = 3 inches on larger hook
To save time, take time to check gauge.

## PATTERN NOTES

Join with slip stitch unless otherwise stated.
On Assembly Diagram first letter indicates color used for Round 1 of motif. Second letter indicates color used for Round 2 of Motif. Color A is used for Round 3 of all motifs.

## FIRST ROW
## FIRST MOTIF

**Rnd 1:** With larger hook and F, ch 5, join to form a ring, ch 3 (counts as dc), dc in ring, ch 1, [(2 dc, ch 2, 2 dc) in ring (corner), ch 1] 3 times, 2 dc in ring, ch 2, join to 3rd ch of beg ch-3 to form last corner. Fasten off.

**Rnd 2:** Attach E in any ch-1 sp, ch 3, dc in same sp, [(3 dc, ch 3, 3 dc) in next corner ch-2 sp, 2 dc in next ch-1 sp] 3 times, (3 dc, ch 3, 3 dc) in next ch-2 corner sp, join in 3rd ch of beg ch-3.

**Rnd 3:** With smaller hook, join A with sc in any ch-3 corner sp, 2 sc in same sp, sc in each st around working 3 sc in each corner ch-3 sp, join in first sc. Fasten off.

## SECOND MOTIF

Referring to Assembly Diagram for colors (see Pattern Notes) and placement, work same as Rnds 1 and 2 of First Motif.

**Rnd 3 (joining rnd):** With smaller hook, join A with sc in any ch-3 corner sp, holding working motif and adjacent motif with WS tog and working through lps of both motifs at same time, 2 sl sts in corresponding

|         |     |     |     |     |     |     |     |     |     |     |
| ------- | --- | --- | --- | --- | --- | --- | --- | --- | --- | --- |
| Row 12  | A/C | G/H | C/F | F/B | D/A | B/G | A/F | H/D | E/F | G/H |
| Row 11  | G/A | C/E | F/D | D/C | B/H | A/C | H/B | E/A | G/C | C/D |
| Row 10  | C/F | F/B | D/A | B/G | A/F | H/D | E/F | G/H | C/B | F/A |
| Row 9   | F/D | D/C | B/H | A/C | H/B | E/A | G/C | C/D | F/E | D/C |
| Row 8   | D/A | B/G | A/F | H/D | E/F | G/H | C/B | F/A | D/G | B/A |
| Row 7   | B/H | A/C | H/B | E/A | G/C | C/D | F/E | D/C | B/F | A/D |
| Row 6   | A/F | H/D | E/F | G/H | C/B | F/A | D/G | B/A | A/B | H/F |
| Row 5   | H/B | E/A | G/C | C/D | F/E | D/C | B/F | A/D | H/A | E/B |
| Row 4   | E/F | G/H | C/B | F/A | D/G | B/A | A/B | H/F | E/D | G/C |
| Row 3   | G/C | C/D | F/E | D/C | B/F | A/D | H/A | E/B | G/H | C/B |
| Row 2   | C/B | F/A | D/G | B/A | A/B | H/F | E/D | G/C | C/A | F/E |
| Row 1   | F/E | D/C | B/F | D/C | H/A | E/B | G/H | C/B | F/D | D/G |

**Playful Colors**
Assembly Diagram

Continued on page 110

# BALL GAME

Design by Joyce Nordstrom

## FINISHED SIZE

Approximately 36 inches across

## MATERIALS

- Lion Brand Baby Soft (5 oz/459 yds/140g per skein): 1 skein each #100 white (A), #184 melon (B), #176 spring green (C) and #158 buttercup (D)
- Size H/8/5mm crochet hook or size necessary to obtain gauge

## GAUGE

Motif = 4½ inches across

To save time, take time to check gauge.

## SPECIAL STITCHES

For **cluster (cl):** Keeping last lp of each dc on hook, 4 dc in st or sp indicated, yo and draw through all 5 lps on hook.

For **joining ch-3 sp:** Ch 1, sl st in corresponding corner ch-3 sp of adjacent motif, ch 1.

## PATTERN NOTE

Join with slip stitch unless otherwise stated.

## FIRST MOTIF

**Rnd 1 (RS):** With C, ch 4, join to form a ring, ch 1, [sc in ring] 12 times, join in first sc. *(12 sc)*

**Rnd 2:** Ch 1, sc in same sc, [ch 5, sc in next sc] 11 times; ch 3, join with dc in first sc to form last ch-5 sp.

**Rnd 3:** Sl st in sp formed by joining dc, ch 3 *(counts as dc),* keeping last lp of each dc on hook, 3 dc in same sp *(beg cl),* [ch 3, **cl** *(see Special Stitches)* in next ch-5 lp] 11 times, ch 3, join in top of beg cl.

**Rnd 4:** Sl st in next ch-3 sp, ch 3, 3 dc in same sp; dc in top of next cl, 4 dc in next ch-3 sp, ch 3 *(corner),* *4 dc in next sp, dc in top of next cl, 4 dc in

next ch-3 sp, ch 3 *(corner);* rep from * 4 times more; join in 3rd ch of beg ch-3. Fasten off.

**Rnd 5:** Attach A, in any corner ch-3 sp, ch 3 *(counts as hdc and ch-1 sp),* *hdc in next dc, [ch 1, sk next dc, hdc in next dc] 4 times, ch 1**, (hdc, ch 3, hdc) in corner ch-3 sp ch 1; rep from * 5 times more, ending last rep at **, hdc in beg ch-3 corner, ch 3; join in 2nd ch of beg ch-3. Fasten off.

## SECOND MOTIF

Referring to Assembly Diagram for color and placement, work same as Rnds 1–4 of First Motif.

**Rnd 5 (joining rnd):** Attach A, in any corner ch-3 sp, ch 3 *(counts as hdc and a ch-1 sp),* hdc in next dc, [ch 1, sk next dc, hdc in next dc] 4 times, ch 1, (hdc, **joining ch-3 sp** *{see Special Stitches},* hdc) in corner ch-3 sp, ch 1; sl st in next ch-1 sp of adjacent motif, hdc in next dc on working motif, ch 1, [sl st in next ch-1 sp of adjacent motif, sk next dc on working motif, hdc in next dc, ch 1] 4 times, (hdc, joining ch-3 sp, hdc) in next corner ch-3 sp, ch 1, *hdc in next dc, [ch 1, sk next dc, hdc in next dc] 4 times, ch 1**, (hdc, ch 3, hdc) in next corner ch-3 sp, ch 1; rep from * 3 times more, ending last rep at **, hdc in beg ch-3 corner, ch 3; join in 2nd ch of beg ch-3. Fasten off.

## REMAINING MOTIFS

Referring to Assembly Diagram for color and placement, work as for Second Motif joining to adjacent motifs in similar manner.

## BORDER

**Rnd 1:** With RS facing, attach A in corner ch-3 sp indicated on Assembly Diagram, ch 4 *(counts as dc and ch-1 sp),* *[sk next hdc, dc in ch-1 sp, ch 1] 6 times, [pull up lp in next corner ch-3 corner sp, yo

and draw through 2 lps on hook] twice, yo and draw through all 3 lps on hook *(dec),* [ch 1, sk next hdc, dc in next ch-1 sp] 6 times, (dc, ch 3, dc) in next corner ch-3 sp *(corner);* rep from * around working dec over corner ch-3 sps of motif joinings and corner in each outer ch-3 corner sp; join in 3rd ch of beg ch-4. Turn.

**Rnd 2:** Sl st in next ch-1 sp, ch 2, hdc in same sp, 2 hdc in each ch-1 sp to next outer corner, (2 hdc, ch 2, 2 hdc) in corner ch-3 sp, 2 hdc in each ch-1 sp before next inner corner dec, pull up lp in each of next 2 ch-1 sps, yo and draw through all 3 lps on hook *(sc dec),* rep from * around, working (2 hdc, ch 2, 2 hdc) in each outside corner ch-3 sp and sc dec at each inner corner; join in 2nd ch of beg ch-2. Fasten off and weave in all ends. 🐾

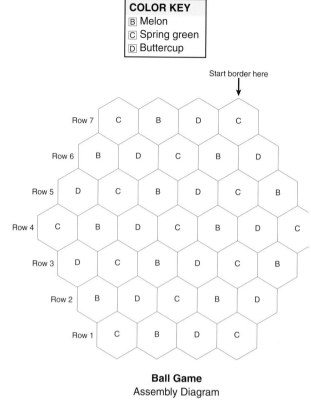

**Ball Game**
Assembly Diagram

# PLAYFUL COLORS Continued from page 106

corner, sl st in each st to next corner, 2 sl sts in next corner, sc in same corner on working motif, [sc in each st to next corner, 3 sc in corner ch-3 sp] twice, sc in each st to beg corner, join in first sc. Fasten off.

## REMAINING MOTIFS
Referring to Assembly Diagram for colors *(see Pattern Notes)* and placement, work rem motifs for First Row in same manner as for Second Motif.

## REMAINING ROWS
Complete rem rows as for First Row joining to adjacent motifs and previous row in similar manner.

## EDGING
Hold with RS facing and one short side at top, with smaller hook attach A with sc in 2nd sc in upper right-hand corner, 2 sc in same sp, sc in each st working 3 sc in each corner around, join in first sc.

## FRINGE
Sl st in next sc, ch 30, *sc in next sc, ch 30, sl st in same st; rep from * around, join to first sc. Fasten off and weave in all ends. 🐾

# SUNSHINE & LACE

Design by Tammy Hildebrand

## FINISHED SIZE

Approximately 36 x 54 inches

## MATERIAL

- Red Heart Classic medium (worsted) weight yarn (3.5 oz/198 yds/100g per skein): 5 skeins #1 white (A), 1 skein each #730 grenadine (B), #48 teal (C) and #230 yellow (D)
- Size I/9/5.5mm crochet hook or size needed to obtain gauge

## GAUGE

Motif = 9½ inches square
To save time, take time to check gauge.

## SPECIAL STITCHES

For **cross-stitch (cross-st):** Sk next st, dc in next st, ch 3, dc in skipped st.

For **joining cross-st:** Sk next st, dc in next st, ch 1, drop lp from hook, insert hook in center ch of corresponding ch-3 on adjacent motif, pull dropped lp through, ch 1, dc in skipped st.

For **joining ch-3 sp:** Ch 1, drop lp from hook, insert hook in center ch of corresponding ch-3 sp on adjacent motif, pull dropped lp through, ch 1.

For **joining ch-5 sp:** Ch 2, drop lp from hook, insert hook in center ch of corresponding ch-5 sp on adjacent motif, pull dropped lp through, ch 2.

## PATTERN NOTE

Join with slip stitch unless otherwise stated.

## FIRST MOTIF

**Rnd 1:** With D, ch 4, join to form a ring, ch 4 *(counts as dc and ch-1 sp),* [dc in ring, ch 1] 11 times, join in 3rd ch of beg ch-4. Fasten off. *(12 dc)*

**Rnd 2:** Attach B with sc in any ch-1 sp, sc in next ch-1 sp, (dc, ch 3, dc) in next ch-1 sp *(corner),* *sc in each of next 2 ch-1 sps, (dc, ch 3, dc) in next ch-1 sp *(corner);* rep from * twice more, join in first sc. Fasten off.

**Rnd 3:** Attach C in any corner ch-3 sp, ch 3 *(counts as dc),* (dc, ch 3, 2 dc) in same sp, dc in next 4 sts, *(2 dc, ch 3, 2 dc) in next corner ch-3 sp, dc in next 4 sts; rep from * twice more, join in 3rd ch of beg ch-3. Fasten off.

**Rnd 4:** Working in sps between sts, join D with sc between 3rd and 4th dc of any 4-dc group on any side, (ch 3, sc) in same sp, sk next 2 dc, (sc, ch 3, sc) in next sp, working over ch-3 corner sp of Rnd 3 in corner ch-3 sp of Rnd 2 (tr, ch 5, tr) in next ch-3 sp, *[sk next 2 dc, (sc, ch 3, sc) in next sp] 3 times, working over ch-3 corner sp of Rnd 3 in corner ch-3 sp of Rnd 2 (tr, ch 5, tr) in next ch-3 sp; rep from * twice more, sk next 2 dc, (sc, ch 3, sc) in next sp, join in first sc. Fasten off.

**Rnd 5:** Attach A with sc in any corner ch-5 sp, 6 sc in same sp, [3 sc in next ch-3 sp] 3 times, *7 sc in next ch-5 sp, [3 sc in next ch-3 sp] 3 times; rep from * twice more, join in first sc.

**Rnd 6:** Sl st in next 2 sc, ch 4, dc in same st, (dc, ch 1, dc) in each of next 2 sts, sk next 2 sts, [(dc, ch 1, dc) in sp before next 3-sc group] 3 times, (dc, ch 1, dc) in sp before next 7-sc group, *sk next 2 sts, (dc, ch 1, dc) in each of next 3 sts, sk next 2 sts, (dc, ch 1, dc) in sp before next 3-sc group] 3 times, (dc, ch 1, dc) in sp before next 7-sc group; rep from * twice more, join in first sc. Fasten off.

**Rnd 7:** Attach B in any ch-1 corner sp, ch 5 *(counts as a dc and ch-2 sp),* dc in same sp, [sc in next 2 dc, ch 1, sk next ch-1 sp] 6 times, sc in next 2 dc, *(dc, ch 2, dc) in next ch-1 sp, [sc in next 2 dc, ch 1, sk next ch-1 sp] 6 times, sc in next 2 sts; rep from * twice more, join in 3rd ch of beg-ch 5. Fasten off.

**Rnd 8:** Working **back lps** only, join A in first ch of any ch-2 corner, ch 6 *(counts as dc and ch-3 sp)*, dc in next ch, dc in next 16 sts skipping ch-1 sps, *dc in next ch, ch 3, dc in next ch, dc in next 16 sts skipping ch-1 sps; rep from * twice more, join in 3rd ch of beg ch-6.

**Rnd 9:** Sl st in next ch-3 sp, ch 6, (dc, ch 5, dc, ch 3, dc) in same sp, [**cross-st** *(see Special Stitches)* over next 2 sts] 9 times, *(dc, ch 3, dc, ch 5, dc, ch 3, dc) in next ch-3 sp, [cross-st over next 2 sts] 9 times; rep from * twice more, join in 3rd ch of beg ch-6. Fasten off.

## SECOND MOTIF

Referring to Assembly Diagram for placement, work same as Rnds 1–8 of First Motif.

**Rnd 9 (joining rnd):** Sl st in next ch-3 sp, (ch 6, dc, **joining ch-5 sp** *{see Special Stitches}*, dc, **joining ch-3 sp** *{see Special Stitches}* dc) in same sp, [**joining cross-st** *(see Special Stitches)* over next 2 sts] 9 times, (dc, joining ch-3 sp, dc, joining ch-5 sp, dc, ch 3, dc) in next ch-3 sp, [cross-st over next 2 sts] 9 times, *(dc, ch 3, dc, ch 5, dc, ch 3, dc) in next ch-3 sp, [cross-st over next 2 sts] 9 times; rep from * once more, join in 3rd ch of beg ch-6. Fasten off.

## REMAINING MOTIFS

Referring to Assembly Diagram for placement, work rem motifs as for Second Motif joining to adjacent motifs in similar manner and making sure all 4-corner joinings are secure.

## BORDER

**Rnd 1:** Attach A with sc in any corner ch-5 sp, 2 sc in same sp, *(dc, ch 1, dc) in each ch-3 sp to motif joining, tr in center of joining, (dc, ch 1, dc) in each ch-3 sp to next corner ch-5 sp, 3 sc in ch-5 sp; rep from * twice more, (dc, ch 1, dc) in each ch-3 sp to motif joining, tr in motif joining, (dc, ch 1, dc) in each ch-3 sp to beg corner, join in first sc. Fasten off.

**Rnd 2:** Attach B with sc in first sc of any 3-sc corner, *sc in next 2 sc, [(ch 1, sk next ch-1 sp, sc in next 2 sts) to last ch-1 sp before tr, ch 1, sk next ch-1 sp, sc in next st, ch 1, sk next tr, sc in next st] to last

motif before 3-sc corner, sk next ch-1 sp, sc in next st, ch 1, sk next tr, sc in next st, (ch 1, sk next ch-1 sp, sc in next 2 sts) to 2nd sc of next 3-sc corner, sc in next sc, rep from * around ending last rep without working last sc, join in first sc. Fasten off.

**Rnd 3:** Working in **back lps** only, join A in center st of any corner, ch 3, (dc, ch 2, 2 dc) in same st, dc in each st to center st of next corner skipping ch-1 sps, [(2 dc, ch 2, 2 dc) in center st of next corner, dc in each st to center st of next corner skipping ch-1 sps] to end, join 3rd ch beg ch-3.

**Rnd 4:** Sl st in ch-2 sp, ch 6, dc in same sp, (cross-st over next 2 sts) to next corner ch-2 sp, *(dc, ch 3, dc) in next ch-2 sp, (cross-st over next 2 sts) to next ch-2 sp; rep from * around, join in 3rd ch of beg ch-6. Fasten off and weave in ends. ꙮ

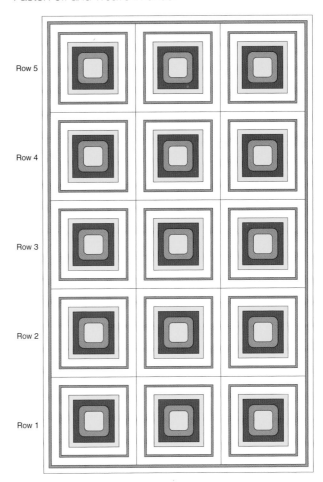

**Sunshine & Lace**
Assembly Diagram

# MAKE ME SMILE

Design by Nanette Seale

## FINISHED SIZE
Approximately 47 x 55 inches

## MATERIALS LIST
- Red Heart Hokey Pokey medium (worsted) weight yarn (4 oz/222 yds/113g per skein): 2 skeins each #7114 lime (A), #7106 light plum (B), #7110 spearmint (C), #7108 tangerine (D), #7107 bubblegum (E), #7113 periwinkle (F)
- Red Heart Classic medium (worsted) weight yarn (3.5 oz/198 yds/99g per skein): 1 skein #12 black
- Size H/8/5mm crochet hook, or size needed to obtain gauge

## GAUGE
Motif = 5½ inches across
To save time, take time to check gauge.

## SPECIAL STITCHES
For **shell:** (2 dc, ch 3, 2 dc) in st or sp indicated.
For **V-stitch (V-st):** (dc, ch 1, dc) in st or sp indicated.

## PATTERN NOTE
Join with slip stitch unless otherwise stated.

## FIRST MOTIF
**Rnd 1:** With A, make slip knot lp on hook, ch 3 *(counts as dc),* 11 dc in lp, join in 3rd ch of beg ch-3. Tighten lp. *(12 sts)*
**Rnd 2:** Ch 3, dc in same st, 2 dc in each dc, join in 3rd ch of beg ch-3. *(24 sts)*
**Rnd 3:** Ch 3, dc in same st, add st, *dc in next dc, 2 dc in next dc; rep from * around, join in 3rd ch of beg ch-3. *(36 sts)*
**Rnd 4:** Ch 3, dc in same st, *dc in next 2 dc, 2 dc

in next dc, rep from * around, join in 3rd ch of beg ch-3. *(48 sts)*
**Rnd 5:** Ch 3, (dc, ch 3, 2 dc) in same st *(beg shell),* * sk next 3 dc, **shell** *(see Special Stitches)* in next dc; rep from * around, join in 3rd ch of beg ch-3. Fasten off. *(12 shells)*

## SECOND MOTIF
Referring to Assembly Diagram for color and placement, work same as First Motif through Rnd 4.
**Rnd 5 (joining rnd):** Ch 3, dc in same st, ch 1, sl st in ch-3 sp of corresponding shell on adjacent motif, ch 1, 2 dc in same st on working motif, *sk next 3 dc, 2 dc in next dc, ch 1, sl st in corresponding ch-3 sp of next shell on adjacent motif, ch 1, 2 dc in same dc on working motif; rep from * once more, [sk next 3 dc, (2 dc, ch 3, 2 dc) in next dc] 8 times, join in 3rd ch of beg ch-3. Fasten off.

## ADDITIONAL MOTIFS
Referring to Assembly Diagram for color and placement, work same as for Second Motif joining to 3 shells of adjacent motifs in similar manner.

## FACES
For **mouth:** With black sl st across 15 sts between Rnds 3 and 4. Fasten off
For **eyes:** With black make slip knot lp on hook, ch 1, 9 hdc in lp, join in first hdc, tighten lp. Fasten off. Sew eyes to motif over Rnds 2 and 3. Weave in ends.

## FILLER MOTIFS
*Note: Filler motifs fill sp where 4 motifs are joined tog.*
**Rnd 1:** With F make slip knot lp on hook, ch 1, 6 sc in lp, join in first sc. Tighten lp.
**Rnd 2 (joining rnd):** Ch 3, dc in same sp, sl st

in ch-2 sp of corresponding shell on adjacent motif, ch 1, 2 dc in same sp on working motif, *sl st in sp between shells on adjacent motif, ch 1, 2 dc in next st on working motif, sl st in next ch-2 shell sp of adjacent motif, ch 1, 2 dc in same st on working motif; rep from * around, join in 3rd ch of beg ch-3.

## BORDER

**Rnd 1:** Referring to Assembly Diagram, attach F in ch-2 sp indicated on motif in upper right-hand corner, ch 3, dc in same sp, [**V-st** *(see Special Stitches)* between shells, shell in ch-3 sp of next shell] 7 times,

*sk the joined shell of next motif, [V-st between shells, shell in ch-3 sp of next shell] 4 times; rep from *, working additional shells and V-sts around outer corners, join in 3rd ch of beg ch-3.

**Rnd 2:** Sl st in next dc and in next ch-3 sp, ch 3, (dc, ch 3, 2 dc) in same sp, *(dc, ch 2, dc) in ch-1 sp of each V-st, shell in ch-3 sp of each shell; rep from * around, join in 3rd ch of beg ch-3.

**Rnd 3:** Sl st in next dc and in next ch-3 sp, ch 3, (2 dc, ch 1, 3 dc) in same sp, *(dc, ch 1, dc) in ch-2 sp of each V-st, (3 dc, ch 1, 3 dc) in each shell; rep from * around, join in 3rd ch of beg ch-3. Fasten off and weave in all ends. ❧

**COLOR KEY**
- A Lime
- B Light Plum
- C Spearmint
- D Tangerine
- E Bubblegum
- F Periwinkle

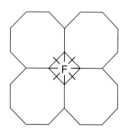

Filler Motif

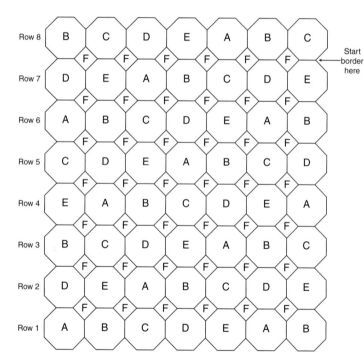

**Make Me Smile**
Assembly Diagram

# PINK PETALS

Design by Tammy Hildebrand

## FINISHED SIZE
Approximately 39 x 55 inches

## MATERIALS
- Bernat Cottontots medium (worsted) weight yarn (3 oz/150 yds/85g per skein): 10 skeins #91422 very berry (A)
- Bernat Cottontots medium (worsted) weight yarn (4 oz/ 200 yds/113g per skein): 2 skeins each #90421 strawberry (B) and #90005 wonder white (C)
- Size I hook or size needed to obtain gauge

## GAUGE
Motif = 7½ inches square

## SPECIAL STITCHES
For **joining ch-3 sp:** Ch 1, drop lp from hook, insert hook in center ch of corresponding ch-3 sp on adjacent motif, pull dropped lp through, ch 1.

For **joining ch-5 sp:** Ch 2, drop lp from hook, insert hook in center ch of corresponding ch-5 sp on adjacent motif, pull dropped lp through, ch 2.

## PATTERN NOTE
Join with slip stitch unless otherwise stated.

## FIRST MOTIF
**Rnd 1:** With A, ch 4, join to form ring, ch 4 *(counts as dc and ch-1 sp)*, dc in ring, [(dc, ch 1, dc) in ring] 7 times, join in 3rd ch of beg ch-4.

**Rnd 2:** Sl st in next ch-1 sp, ch 1, (sc, ch 3, sc) in same sp and in each ch-1 sp around, join in first sc. Fasten off.

**Rnd 3:** Attach B in any ch-3 sp, ch 3 *(counts as dc),* 4 dc in same sp *(beg shell),* 5 dc in each ch-3 sp *(shell)* around, join in 3rd ch of beg ch-3. Fasten off. *(8 shells)*

**Rnd 4:** Attach C in sp between any 2 shells, ch 4, dc in same sp, sk next 2 sc, dc in **back lp** of next sc, (tr, ch 1, tr, ch 3, tr, ch 1, tr) in sp before next shell *(corner),* *sk next 2 sc, dc in **back lp** of next sc, (dc, ch 1, dc) in sp before next shell, sk next 2 sc, dc in **back lp** of next sc, (tr, ch 1, tr, ch 3, tr, ch 1, tr) in sp before next shell *(corner);* rep from * twice more, sk next 2 sc, dc in **back lp** of next sc, join in 3rd ch of beg ch-4. Fasten off.

**Rnd 5:** Attach A with sc in any corner ch-3 sp, 4 sc in same sp, [3 sc in next ch-1 sp, 3 sc in next dc] twice, 3 sc in next ch-1 sp, *5 sc in next ch-3 sp, [3 sc in next ch-1 sp, 3 sc in next dc] twice, 3 sc in next ch-1 sp; rep from * twice more, join in first sc.

**Rnd 6:** Sl st in next 2 sc, ch 6 *(counts as dc and ch-3 sp),* (dc, ch 5, dc, ch 3, dc) in same st, sk next 2 sc, working in sps between 3-sc groups, [(dc, ch 3, dc) in sp before next 3-sc group] 6 times, *sk next 2 sc, (dc, ch 3, dc, ch 5, dc, ch 3, dc) in next sc, sk next 2 sc, [(dc, ch 3, dc) in sp before next 3-sc group) 6 times; rep from * twice more, sk next 2 sc, join in 3rd ch of beg ch-6. Fasten off.

## SECOND MOTIF
Referring to Assembly Diagram for placement, work same as Rnds 1–5 of First Motif.

**Rnd 6 (joining rnd):** Sl st in next 2 sts, ch 6 *(counts as dc and ch-3 sp),* (dc, **joining ch-5 sp** *{see Special Stitches},* dc, **joining ch-3 sp** *{see Special Stitches},* dc) in same st, sk next 2 sc, working in sps between 3-sc groups, [(dc, joining ch-3 sp, dc) in sp before next 3-sc group] 6 times, sk next 2 sc, [(dc, joining ch-3 sp, dc, joining ch-5 sp, dc, ch 3, dc) in next st, sk next 2 sc, (dc, ch 3, dc in sp before next

3-sc group] 6 times, *sk next 2 sc, (dc, ch 3, dc, ch 5, dc, ch 3, dc) in next sc, [sk next 2 sc, (dc, ch 3, dc) in sp before next 3-sc group] 6 times; rep from * once more, join in 3rd ch of beg ch-6. Fasten off.

## REMAINING MOTIFS

Referring to Assembly Diagram for placement, work rem motifs in same manner as Second Motif joining to adjacent motifs in similar manner and making sure all 4-corner joinings are secure.

## BORDER

Hold with RS facing and one short edge at top, attach B with sc in ch-5 sp in upper right-hand corner, 4 sc in same sp, *sc in next ch-3 sp, 3 sc in each of next 7 ch-3 sps, [(dc, ch 1, dc) in center of motif joining, 3 sc in each of next 8 ch-sps] 3 times, (dc, ch 1, dc) in center of motif joining, 3 sc in each of next 7 ch-3 sps, sc in next ch-3 sp, 5 sc in next ch-5 sp, sc in next ch-3 sp, 3 sc in each of next 7 ch-3 sps; rep between [ ] 5 times, (dc, ch 1, dc) in center of motif joining, 3 sc in each of next 7 ch-3 sps, sc in next ch-3 sp**, 5 sc in next ch sp; rep from * around ending last rep at **, join first sc.
Fasten off and weave in ends. 🐾

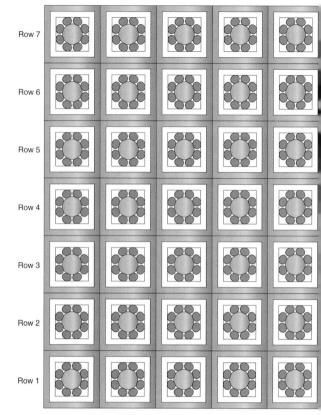

**Pink Petals**
Assembly Diagram

# SEASONAL PLEASURES

These afghans take their inspiration from favorite holidays, like Christmas and Valentine's Day, and from the seasons, spring and autumn.

**SKILL LEVEL**
EASY

**YARN WEIGHT**
4 MEDIUM

# BE MY VALENTINE

Design by Donna Collinsworth

## FINISHED SIZE
Approximately 48 x 68 inches

## MATERIALS
- Red Heart Super Saver medium (worsted) weight yarn (8 oz/452 yds/226g per skein): 5 skeins #313 aran (A), 2 skeins each #374 country rose (B) and #372 rose pink (C)
- Size G/6/4mm crochet hook or size needed to obtain gauge

## GAUGE
Motif = 2 inches square
To save time, take time to check gauge.

## PATTERN NOTES
Join with slip stitch unless otherwise indicated.

## FIRST ROW
### FIRST MOTIF
**Rnd 1:** With C, ch 4, join to form a ring, ch-1, [3 sc in ring, ch 2] 4 times, join in first sc.

**Rnd 2:** Ch 3 *(counts as dc)*, dc in next 2 sc, *(dc, ch 2, dc) in next ch-2 sp *(corner)*, dc next 3 sc; rep from * 3 times more, (dc, ch 2, dc) in next ch-2 sp *(corner)*, join in 3rd ch of beg ch-3. Fasten off.

### SECOND MOTIF
**Rnd 1:** Work same as Rnd 1 of First Motif.
**Rnd 2 (joining rnd):** Ch 3 *(counts as dc)*, dc in next 2 sc, *dc in next ch-2 sp, ch 1, sc in corresponding corner ch-2 sp on adjacent motif, ch 1, dc in same sp on working motif *(corner)*, dc next 3 sc; rep from * once more, (dc, ch 2, dc) in next ch-2 sp *(corner)*, dc in next 3 sc, (dc, ch 2, dc) in next ch-2 sp *(corner)*, join in 3rd ch of beg ch-3. Fasten off.

## REMAINING MOTIFS
Referring to Assembly Diagram for color and placement, work rem motifs in same manner as for Second Motif.

## ADDITIONAL ROWS
***Note:*** *Some of the additional rows contain Two-Color Motifs as shown by a diagonally split box on the Assembly Diagram and 4-Patch Motifs as indicated on Assembly Diagram. When joining Two-Color Motifs and 4-Patch Motifs to adjacent motifs, take care to position the colors correctly.*

## TWO-COLOR MOTIF
**Rnd 1:** With A, ch 4, join to form a ring, ch 1, (3 sc, ch 2, 3 sc) in ring, ch 1, change to B by drawing lp though, working over A, ch 1, (3 sc, ch 2, 3 sc, ch 1) in ring, change to A by drawing lp through, ch 1, join in first sc.
***Note:*** *Referring to Assembly Diagram for color placement join to adjacent motifs in corresponding corner ch-2 sps as for Rnd 2 of Second Motif.*
**Rnd 2:** With A and working over B, ch 3 *(counts as dc)*, dc next 2 sc, (dc, ch 2, dc) in next ch-2 sp *(corner)*, dc next 3 sc, dc in next ch-2 sp *(corner)*, with B, ch 2, dc in same sp, working over A, dc in next 3 sc, (dc, ch 2, dc) in next ch-2 sp *(corner)*, dc next 3 sc, dc in next ch-2 sp *(corner)*, with A, ch 2, dc in same sp, join in 3rd ch of beg ch-3. Fasten off.

## 4-PATCH MOTIF
### FIRST SMALL SQUARE
With C, ch 4, join to form a ring, ch 1, (3 sc, ch 2) 4 times in ring, join in first sc. Fasten off.

## SECOND SMALL SQUARE

With A, ch 4, join to form a ring, ch 1, 3 sc in ring, ch 1, sc in corresponding corner of first square, 3 sc in ring, ch 1, sc in corresponding corner of first square, (3 sc, ch 2) twice in ring, join in first sc. Fasten off.

## THIRD SMALL SQUARE

Work as First Small Square joining to adjacent small squares.

Continued on page 126

**COLOR KEY**
- ☐ A
- ◼ B
- ▨ C
- ▨ 4-patch motif
- ◺ Two-color motif

Row 1

**Be My Valentine**
Assembly Diagram

**SKILL LEVEL**
EASY

**YARN WEIGHT**
4
MEDIUM

# SPRING BOUQUET

Design by Kathleen Garen

## FINISHED SIZE
Approximately 48 x 62 inches

## MATERIALS
- Caron Simply Soft medium (worsted) weight yarn (6 oz/315 yds/170g per skein): 2 skeins each #2706 red (B), #2601 white (A) and #2697 royale (C)
- Caron Simple Soft medium (worsted) weight yarn 15 oz assorted colors
- Size K/10.5/6.5mm crochet hook or size needed to obtain gauge

## GAUGE
Motif = 3 inches
To save time, take time to check gauge.

## SPECIAL STITCHES
For **cluster (cl):** Keeping last lp of each dc on hook, 2 dc in st or sp indicated, yo and draw through all 3 lps on hook.
For **shell:** (Dc, ch 1, dc) in sp or st indicated.
For **small shell:** (Dc, ch 1, dc, ch 1, dc) in sp or st indicated.

## PATTERN NOTES
Join with slip stitch unless otherwise stated.
Sample afghan was made with assorted lighter colored motifs in the center and darker motifs of the same color used around the outer edge to border the afghan.

## FIRST MOTIF
With desired color, ch 5, join to form a ring, [sc in ring, ch 7, sc in ring, ch 11] 4 times, join in first sc. Fasten off.

## SECOND MOTIF
With desired color, ch 5, join to form a ring, sc in ring, ch 7, sc in ring, ch 11, sc in ring, ch 7, sc in ring, [ch 5, remove hook, insert hook in 6th ch of corresponding ch-11 lp on adjacent motif and draw dropped lp through, ch 5, sc in ring], ch 3, remove hook, insert hook in 4th ch of corresponding ch-7 on adjacent motif and draw dropped lp through, ch 3, sc in ring; rep between [ ] once, ch 7, sc in ring, ch 11, sc in ring, join in first sc. Fasten off.

## REMAINING MOTIFS
Work rem motif with desired color as for Second Motif, joining to all adjacent motifs in similar manner.

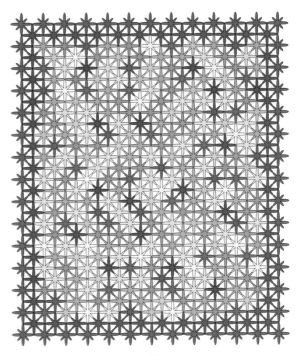

**Spring Bouquet**
Assembly Diagram

## BORDER

**Rnd 1:** Hold with RS facing and 1 short end at top, attach A in 6th ch of ch-11 sp in top right-hand corner, ch 4 *(counts as dc and ch-1 sp),* **shell** *(see Special Stitches)* in same sp, **small shell** *(see Special Stitches)* in 4th ch of next ch-7 sp, **cl** *(see Special Stitches)* in motif joining, *small shell in 4th ch of next ch-7 sp, (dc, ch 1) 3 times in 6th ch of next ch-11 sp, dc in same sp, small shell in 4th ch of next ch-7 sp, cl in motif joining; rep from * around, working in additional ch-7 and ch-11 sps at corners in similar manner; join in 3rd ch of beg ch-4.

**Rnd 2:** 2 sc in next ch-1 sp, 3 sc in next ch-1 sp, 2 sc in next ch-1 sp, sc between shells, 2 sc in each of next 2 ch-1 sps, sk next cl, continue around in similar manner working 2 sc in each sc of small shell, sc in sp between shells, 2 sc in first ch-1 sp of shell, 3 sc in center ch-1 sp of shell and 2 sc in last ch-1 sp of shell and skipping cls, join in first sc. Turn.

**Rnd 3:** Working in **back lps** only, sl st in each st, join in first sc.

Fasten off and weave in all ends. ❧

# BE MY VALENTINE Continued from page 123

### FOURTH SMALL SQUARE

Work as Second Small Square joining to adjacent small squares.

### REMAINING MOTIFS

Referring to Assembly Diagram for type of motif, color and placement, make additional Motifs, Two-Color Motifs and 4-Patch Motifs and join in similar manner to adjacent motifs.

### BORDER

**Rnd 1:** Hold with RS facing and one short end at top, attach B in ch-2 sp in upper right-hand corner, ch 1, sc in each dc and corner sp around and working (2 sc, ch 2, 2 sc) in each outer corner ch-2 sp around, join in first sc.

**Rnd 2:** Ch 3, dc in each sc working (2 dc, ch 2, 2 dc) in each corner, join in 3rd ch of beg ch-3. Fasten off and weave in all ends. ❧

SKILL LEVEL

■■■□
INTERMEDIATE

YARN WEIGHT

④
MEDIUM

# PATRIOT'S PICNIC

Design by Maria Merlino

## FINISHED SIZE
Approximately 42 x 58 inches

## MATERIALS
- Red Heart Classic medium (worsted) weight yarn (3.5 oz/198 yds/100g per skein): 7 skeins #1 white (A), 5 skeins #912 cherry red (B), 3 skeins #853 soft navy (C)
- Size H/8/5mm crochet hook or size required for gauge

## GAUGE
Motif = 8 inches square
To save time, take time to check gauge.

## SPECIAL STITCHES
For **triple crochet cluster (tr cl):** Keeping last lp of each tr on hook, tr in each of next 4 tr, yo and draw through all 5 lps on hook.
For **picot:** Ch 3, sc in 3rd ch from hook.

## PATTERN NOTE
Join with slip stitch unless otherwise stated.

## FIRST MOTIF
**Rnd 1:** With A, ch 6, join to form a ring, ch 4 *(counts as tr),* 3 tr in ring, ch 4, turn, **tr cl** *(see Special Stitches),* turn *(petal),* ch 4, *working behind back of petal just made, 4 tr in ring, ch 4, turn, tr cl over 4 tr just made, turn (petal), ch 4; rep from * 3 times more, join in 4th ch of beg ch-4. *(5 ch-4 sps)* Fasten off.
**Rnd 2:** Attach C in any ch-4 sp, ch 1, 8 sc in same sp *(mark first sc for ease in joining rnd),* 8 sc in each of next 4 ch-4 sps, join in first sc. *(40 sc)*
**Rnd 3:** Ch 3 *(counts as dc),* (2 dc, ch 2, 3 dc) in same sp *(corner),* ch 1, sk next 4 sc, 3 dc in next

sc, ch 1, sk next 4 sc, *(3 dc, ch 2, 3 dc) in next sc *(corner),* ch 1, sk next 4 sc, 3 dc in next sc, ch 1; rep from * twice more, sk next 4 sc, join in 3rd ch of beg ch-3. Fasten off.
**Rnd 4:** Attach A in any corner ch-2 sp, ch 3, 2 dc in same sp, ch 1, [3 dc in next ch-1 sp, ch 1] twice, *(3 dc, ch 2, 3 dc) in next corner ch-2 sp, ch 1, [3 dc in next ch-1 sp, ch 1] twice; rep from * twice more, 3 dc in first ch-2 sp, ch 1, join with sc in 3rd ch of beg ch-3, changing to B. **Do not cut A.**
**Rnd 5:** With B, ch 3, working over joining sc, 2 dc in same sp, ch 1, [3 dc in next ch-1 sp, ch 1] 3 times, *(3 dc, ch 2, 3 dc) in corner ch-2 sp, ch 1, [3 dc in next ch-1 sp, ch 1] 3 times; rep from * twice more, 3 dc in first ch-2 sp, ch 1, join with sc in 3rd ch of beg ch-3, changing to A. **Do not cut B.**
**Rnd 6:** With A, ch 3, working over sc joining, 2 dc in same sp, ch 1, [3 dc in next ch-1 sp, ch 1] 4 times, *(3 dc, ch 2, 3 dc) in corner ch-2 sp, ch 1, [3 dc in next ch-1 sp, ch 1] 4 times; rep from * twice more, 3 dc in first ch-2 sp, ch 1, join with sc in 3rd ch of beg ch-3, changing to B. Fasten off A.
**Rnd 7:** With B, ch 3, working over sc joining, 2 dc in same sp, ch 1, [3 dc in next ch-1 sp, ch 1] 5 times, *(3 dc, ch 2, 3 dc) in corner ch-2 sp, ch 1, [3 dc in next ch-1 sp, ch 1] 5 times; rep from * twice more, 3 dc in first ch-2 sp, ch 2; join in 3rd ch of beg ch-3. Fasten off.

## SECOND MOTIF
Referring to Assembly Diagram for placement, work Rnds 1–6 same as for First Motif.

**Rnd 7 (joining rnd):** With B, ch 3, working over joining sc, 2 dc in same sp, ch 1, [3 dc in next ch-1 sp, ch 1] 5 times, 3 dc in corner ch-2 sp, ch 1, holding working motif and adjacent motif with WS tog, sl st in corresponding corner of adjacent motif, ch 1, 3 dc in same sp on working motif, *ch 1, sl st in corresponding ch-1 sp of adjacent motif, 3 dc in next ch-1 sp on working motif; rep from * to next corner, ch 1, sl st in last ch-1 sp of adjacent motif, 3 dc in next corner ch-2 sp of working motif, ch 1, sl st in corresponding ch-2 sp of adjacent motif, ch 1, 3 dc in same sp on working motif, ch 1, [3 dc in next ch-1 sp, ch 1] 5 times, (3 dc, ch 2, 3 dc) in corner ch-2 sp, [3 dc in next ch-1 sp, ch 1] 5 times, 3 dc in beg corner, ch 2, join in 3rd ch of beg ch-3. Fasten off.

## REMAINING MOTIFS

Referring to Assembly Diagram for placement, work as for Second Motif joining to adjacent motifs in similar manner and making sure all 4-corner joinings are secure.

## BORDER

**Rnd 1:** Attach B in any ch-2 sp, ch 3, (2 dc, ch 2, 3 dc) in same sp, ch 1, *[3 dc in next ch-1 sp, ch 1] 6 times, dc in corner ch-2 sp, dc in motif joining, dc in corner ch-2 sp of next motif, ch 1; rep from * around working (3 dc, ch 2, 3 dc) in each outer corner ch-2 sp, join in 3rd ch of beg ch-3. Fasten off.

**Rnd 2:** Attach A in any corner ch-2 sp, ch 3, (2 dc, ch 2, 3 dc) in same sp, ch 1, *(3 dc, ch 1) in each ch-1 sp to next corner ch-2 sp, (3 dc, ch 2, 3 dc) in next corner ch-2 sp; rep from * around, join in 3rd ch of beg ch-3. Fasten off.

**Rnd 3:** Attach C in any ch-2 corner sp, ch 3, (2 dc, **picot** {see Special Stitches}, 3 dc) in same sp, picot, *(3 dc, picot) in each ch-1 sp, to next corner ch-2 sp, (3 dc, picot, 3 dc) in next ch-2 sp, (3 dc, picot) in each ch-1 sp; rep from * around; join in 3rd ch of beg ch-3. Fasten off and weave in all ends. 🐚

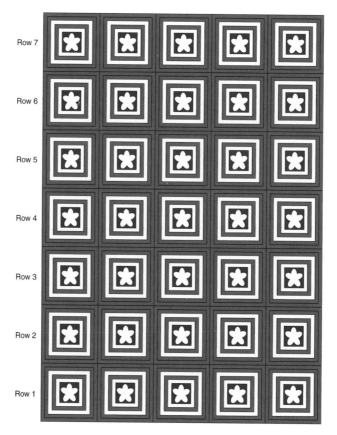

**Patriot's Picnic**
Assembly Diagram

# FALL FOLIAGE

Design by Kathleen Stuart

## FINISHED SIZE
Approximately 52½ x 58 inches

## MATERIALS
- TLC Essentials medium (worsted) weight yarn (6 oz/326 yds/170g per skein): 6 skeins #2220 butter (A), 1 skein each #2915 cranberry (B) and #2254 persimmon (C)
- TLC Essentials medium (worsted) weight yarn (4.5 oz/255 yds/127g per skein): 4 skeins #2958 falling leaves (D)
- Size G/6/4mm crochet hook or size needed to obtain gauge

## GAUGE
Motif = 6 inches across from straight edge to straight edge
To save time, take time to check gauge.

## SPECIAL STITCHES
For **beginning cluster (beg cl):** Ch 2, [yo, insert hook in st or sp indicated, yo and pull up a lp, yo and draw through 2 lps on hook] twice, yo and draw through all 3 lps on hook.

For **cluster (cl):** [Yo, insert hook in st or sp indicated, yo and pull up a lp, yo and draw through 2 lps on hook] 3 times, yo and draw through all 4 lps on hook.

For **picot:** Ch 4, sc in 3rd ch from hook.

## PATTERN NOTE
Join with slip stitch unless otherwise stated.

## FIRST MOTIF (PLAIN MOTIF)
**Rnd 1:** With A, ch 6, join to form lp; ch 1, [2 sc in lp, ch 1] 6 times, join in first sc.

**Rnd 2:** Sl st in next sc and in next ch-1 sp, ch 5 *(counts as dc and ch-2 sp),* dc in same sp, ch 2, *(dc, ch 2, dc) in next ch-1 sp, ch 2, rep from * 4 times more, join 3rd ch of beg ch-5. *(12 dc)*

**Rnd 3:** Ch 1, sc in same ch as joining, *3 sc in next ch-2 sp, sc in next dc; rep from * 10 times more, 3 sc in next ch-2 sp, join in first sc.

**Rnd 4:** Ch 5, dc in same sp *(beg corner),* ch 1, [sk next sc, dc in next sc, ch 1] 3 times, sk next sc, *(dc, ch 2, dc) in next sc *(corner),* ch 1, sk next sc, [dc in next sc, ch 1, sk next sc] 3 times; rep from * 4 times more; join in 3rd ch of beg ch-5. *(30 dc)*

**Rnd 5:** Sl st in next ch-2 sp, ch 5, dc in same sp, [dc in next dc and in next ch-1 sp] 4 times, dc in next dc, *(dc, ch 2, dc) in next corner ch-2 sp, [dc in next dc and in next ch-1 sp) 4 times, dc in next dc; rep from * 4 times more, join in 3rd ch of beg ch-5. *(66 dc)*

**Rnd 6:** Sl st in next dc and in next ch-2 sp, (**beg cl** *{see Special Stitches},* ch 2, **cl** *{see Special Stitches})* in same sp, ch 2, [sk next 2 dc, cl in next dc, ch 2] 3 times, *[cl, ch 2] twice in next ch-2 sp, [sk next 2 dc, cl in next dc, ch 2] 3 times; rep from * 4 times more, join in top of beg cl. Fasten off. *(30 cls)*

**Rnd 7:** Attach D in any corner ch-2 sp; ch 1, 3 sc in same sp, sc in next cl, [2 sc in next ch-2 sp, sc in next cl] 4 times, *3 sc in next corner ch-2 sp, sc in next cl, [2 sc in next ch-2 sp, sc in next cl] 4 times; rep from * 4 times more; join in first sc.

**Rnd 8:** *Sc in next sc, ch 3, sc in same st, [ch 3, sk next sc, sc in next sc] 7 times, ch 3, sk next sc; rep from * around, join in first sc.

## SECOND MOTIF (FLOWER MOTIF)
**Rnd 1:** With C, ch 5; join to form a ring, ch 1, 12 sc in ring. *(12 sc)*

**Rnd 2:** Ch 1, sc in same sc, *(sc, ch 3, 2 dc, **picot**

{see Special Stitches}, ch 1, 2 dc, ch 3, sc) in next sc (petal), sc in next sc; rep from * 4 times more, (sc, ch 3, 2 dc, picot, ch 1, 2 dc, ch 3, sc) in next sc; join in first sc. (6 petals)

**Rnd 3:** Ch 1, sc in same sc, ch 4, sk next petal, [sc in next sc, ch 4, sk next petal] 5 times, join in first sc. Fasten off.

**Rnd 4:** Attach A with sc in any ch-4 sp, 7 sc in same sp, 8 sc in each ch-4 sp; join in first sc. (48 sc)

**Rnd 5:** Ch 5 (counts as dc and ch-2 sp), dc in same st (beg corner), ch 1, [sk next sc, dc in next sc, ch 1] 3 times, sk next sc, *(dc, ch 2, dc) in next sc (corner), ch 1, sk next sc, [dc in next sc, ch 1, sk next sc] 3 times; rep from * 4 times more; join in 3rd ch in beg ch-5. (30 dc)

**Rnd 6:** Sl st in next ch-2 sp, ch 5, dc in same sp, [dc in next dc and in next ch-1 sp] 4 times, dc in next dc, *(dc, ch 2, dc) in next corner ch-2 sp, [dc in next dc and in next ch-1 sp) 4 times, dc in next dc; rep from * 4 times more, join in 3rd ch of beg ch-5. (66 dc)

**Rnd 7:** Sl st in next dc and in next ch-2 sp, (**beg cl** {see Special Stitches}, ch 2, **cl** {see Special Stitches}) in same sp, ch 2, [sk next 2 dc, cl in next dc, ch 2] 3 times, *[cl, ch 2] twice in next ch-2 sp, [sk next 2 dc, cl in next dc, ch 2] 3 times; rep from * 4 times more, join in top of beg cl. Fasten off. (30 cls)

**Rnd 8:** Attach D in any corner ch-2 sp; ch 1, 3 sc in same sp, sc in next cl, [2 sc in next ch-2 sp, sc in next cl] 4 times, *3 sc in next corner ch-2 sp, sc in next cl, [2 sc in next ch-2 sp, sc in next cl] 4 times; rep from * 4 times more; join in first sc.

**Rnd 9 (joining rnd):** Sc in next sc, ch 1, sl st in corresponding corner ch-3 sp of adjacent motif, ch 1, sc in same sc on working motif, [ch 1, sl st in next ch-3 sp adjacent motif, ch 1, sk next sc on working motif, sc in next sc] 8 times, ch 1, sl st in corresponding corner ch-3 sp on adjacent motif, ch 1, sc in same sp on working motif, *[ch 3, sk next sc, sc in next st] 7 times, ch 3, sk next st**, (sc, ch 3, sc) in next sc; rep from * 4 times more, ending last rep at **, join in first sc.

## REMAINING MOTIFS

Referring to Assembly Diagram for motif type, color and placement, work same as for Plain Motif or Flower Motif, joining to adjacent motifs in similar manner on last rnd. ❧

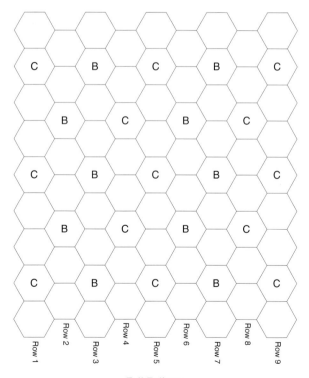

**COLOR KEY**
C Persimmon flower motif
B Cranberry flower motif

**Fall Foliage**
Assembly Diagram

**SKILL LEVEL**
INTERMEDIATE

**YARN WEIGHT**
4 MEDIUM

# POINSETTIA BEAUTIES

Design by Maria Merlino

## FINISHED SIZE

43 x 58 inches

## MATERIALS

- Red Heart Super Saver medium (worsted) weight yarn (8 oz/452 yds/226g per skein): 3 skeins #389 hunter green (A)
- Red Heart Classic medium (worsted) weight yarn (3½ oz/198 yds/99g per skein): 4 skeins #912 cherry red (B), 1 skein #230 yellow (C)
- Size H/8/5mm crochet hook or size needed to obtain gauge
- 5-inch piece of cardboard (for tassels)

## GAUGE

Motif = 8 inches square
To save time, take time to check gauge.

## SPECIAL STITCHES

For **beginning cluster (beg cl):** Ch 3, keeping last lp of each dc on hook, 2 dc in st or sp indicated, yo and draw through all 3 lps on hook.

For **cluster (cl):** Keeping last lp of each dc on hook 3 dc in sp or st indicated, yo and draw through all 4 lps on hook.

For **double triple crochet (dtr):** Yo 4 times, pullup lp in sp or st indicated, [yo, draw through 2 lps on hook] 5 times.

For **picot:** Ch 2, sl st in 2nd ch from hook.

## PATTERN NOTE

Join with slip stitch unless otherwise stated.

## FIRST MOTIF

**Rnd 1:** With C, ch 4, join to form a ring, **beg cl** *(see Special Stitches),* ch 2, [**cl** *(see Special Stitches),* ch 2] 7 times, join in top of beg cl. Fasten off. *(8 cls)*

**Rnd 2:** Attach B in any ch-2 sp, *(ch 4, tr, **dtr** *(see Special Stitches),* **picot** *(see Special Stitches),* dtr, tr, ch 4, sl st) in same sp *(petal),* sl st in next ch-2 sp; rep from * 7 times more. *(8 petals)*

**Rnd 3:** Working behind petals, [ch 4, sl st in sp between petals] 7 times, ch 4, join in sp between petals. Fasten off. *(8 ch-4 sps)*

**Rnd 4:** Attach A in any ch-4 sp, ch 3 *(counts as dc)* 2 dc in same sp, ch 1, 3 dc in next ch-4 sp, *(3 dc, ch 2, 3 dc) in next sp *(corner),* ch 1, 3 dc in in next ch-4 sp, ch 1; rep from * twice more, 3 dc in first ch-4 sp, ch 1, join with sc in 3rd ch beg ch-3 to form last corner ch-2 sp.

**Rnd 5:** Ch 3, working over joining sc, 2 dc in same sp, ch 1, [3 dc, ch 1] in each ch-1 sp to next corner ch-2 sp, *(3 dc, ch 2, 3 dc) in corner ch-2 sp, ch 1, [3 dc, ch 1] in each ch-1 sp to corner, rep from * twice more, 3 dc in first ch-2 sp, ch 1, join with a sc in 3rd ch of beg ch-3 to form last ch-2 sp.

**Rnds 6 & 7:** Rep Rnd 5.

**Rnd 8:** Ch 3, working over joining sc, 2 dc in same sp, ch 1, (3 dc, ch 1), in each ch-1 sp to corner, *(3 dc, ch 2, 3 dc) in corner ch-2 sp, ch 1, (3 dc, ch 1) in each ch-1 sp to corner, rep from * twice more, 3 dc in first ch-2 sp, ch 2, join in 3rd ch of beg ch-3. Fasten off.

## SECOND MOTIF

Referring to Assembly Diagram for placement, work same as Rnds 1–7 of First Motif.

**Rnd 8 (joining rnd):** Ch 3, working over joining sc, 2 dc in same sp, ch 1, (3 dc in next ch-1 sp, ch 1) to corner ch-2 sp, 3 dc in corner ch-2 sp, ch 1, holding working motif and adjacent motif with WS tog, sl st in corresponding ch-2 corner sp of adjacent motif, ch 1, 3 dc in same ch-2 sp on working motif, *ch 1, sl st in corresponding ch-1 sp of adjacent motif, 3 dc in next ch-1 sp on working motif, rep from * to next corner ch-2 sp, ch 1, sl st in corresponding ch-1 sp of adjacent square, 3 dc in corner ch-2 sp of working motif, ch 1, sl st in corresponding ch-2 sp of adjacent square, ch 1, 3 dc in same ch-2 sp of working motif to form a joined corner, ch 1, [3 dc in next ch-1 sp, ch 1] to next corner, (3 dc, ch 2, 3 dc) in corner ch-2 sp, [3 dc in next ch-1 sp, ch 1] to next corner, 3 dc in beg corner, ch 2, join in 3rd ch of beg ch-3. Fasten off.

## REMAINING MOTIFS

Referring to Assembly Diagram for placement, work same as for Second Motif, joining to adjacent motifs in similar manner and making sure all 4-corner joinings are secure.

## SIDE MOTIFS

**Rnd 1:** With A, ch 4, 2 dc in 4th ch from hook, ch 2, [3 dc in same sp, ch 2] twice, 3 dc in same sp, ch 1, sc 4th ch of beg ch-4 to form last ch-2 sp.

**Rnd 2:** Ch 2, 2 dc in same sp, ch 1, *(3 dc, ch 2, 3 dc) in next ch-2 sp, ch 1; rep from * twice more, 3 dc in beg ch-2 sp, ch 1, sc in 3rd ch of beg ch-3.

**Rnd 3 (joining rnd):** Join Side Motif to 2 adjacent motifs in same manner as for motif joining beg in the 4th ch-1 sp of adjacent motifs.

## TASSELS

### MAKE 14.

For **tassel:** Wind A around 5-inch piece of cardboard 25 times. Cut across 1 end. Leave lengths folded. Cut 1 (8-inch) length of C.

**To attach tassel:** Attach A in ch-2 corner point of Side Motif as indicated on Assembly Diagram, ch 3, sl st tightly around folded A yarn lengths, ch 1, sl st in next 3 chs, sl st in beg ch-2 corner. Fasten off. Fold C in half. Tie a square knot 1 inch below fold. Trim ends. Trim tassel to 3½ inches. ❧

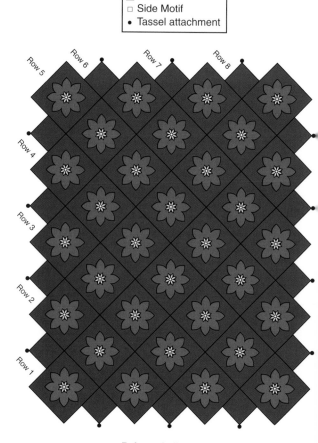

**Poinsettia Beauties**
Assembly Diagram

# MOOD
# MONOCHROME

Sometimes you want an afghan to softly blend in with your decor. These designs can add texture to your room without jarring the senses.

SKILL LEVEL
INTERMEDIATE

YARN WEIGHT
2 FINE

# CHRISTENING ROSE

Design by Maria Merlino

## FINISHED SIZE
Approximately 31 x 40 inches

## MATERIALS
- Red Heart Baby Pompadour super fine (fingering) yarn (1.75 oz/270 yds/50g per skein): 11 skeins #1 white
- Size H/8/5mm crochet hook or size needed to obtain gauge

## GAUGE
Motif = 5½ inches
To save time, take time to check gauge.

## SPECIAL STITCHES
For **joining ch-2 sp:** Ch 1, sl st in corresponding corner ch-2 sp on adjacent motif, ch 1.
For **picot:** Ch 3, sc in 3rd ch from hook.

## PATTERN NOTE
Join with slip stitch unless otherwise stated.

## FIRST MOTIF
**Rnd 1:** Ch 1, join to from a ring, ch 1, 16 sc in ring, join in first sc. (16 sc)
**Rnd 2:** Ch 1, sc in same sc, ch 2, sk next sc, [sc in next sc, ch 2, sk next sc] 7 times, join in first sc.
**Rnd 3:** Sl st in next ch-2 sp, ch 1, (sc, hdc, dc, hdc, sc) in same sp (petal), [(sc, hdc, dc, hdc, sc) in next ch-2 sp (petal)] 7 times. (8 petals)
**Rnd 4:** Ch 3, working behind petals on Rnd 3, sl st around **post** (see Stitch Guide) of next sc on Rnd 2, [ch 3, sl st around post of next sc on Rnd 2] 7 times. (8 ch-3 sps)

**Rnd 5:** Sl st in next ch-3 sp, ch 1, (hdc, dc, 2 tr, dc, hdc) in same sp (petal), [(hdc, dc, 2 tr, dc, hdc) in next ch-3 sp (petal)] 7 times.
**Rnd 6:** Ch 3, working behind petals on Rnd 5, sl st around post of next sl st on Rnd 4, [ch 3, sl st around post of next sl st on Rnd 4] 7 times.
**Rnd 7:** Sl st in next ch-3 sp and in first and 2nd ch of same sp, ch 3 (counts as dc), 2 dc in same lp, ch 1, 3 dc in next ch-3 sp, ch 1, *(3 dc, ch 2, 3 dc) in next ch-3 sp (corner), ch 1, 3 dc in next ch-3 sp, ch 1; rep from * twice more, 3 dc in beg sp, ch 1, join with sc in 3rd ch of beg ch-3 to form beg corner.
**Rnd 8:** Ch 3, 2 dc in sp formed by joining sc, ch 1, [3 dc in next ch-1 sp, ch 1] twice, *(3 dc, ch 2, 3 dc) in corner ch-2 sp, ch 1, [3 dc in next ch-1 sp, ch 1] twice; rep from * twice more, 3 dc in beg sp, ch 1, join with sc in 3rd ch of beg ch-3 to form beg corner.
**Rnd 9:** Ch 3, 2 dc in sp formed by joining sc, ch 1, [3 sc in next ch-1 sp, ch 1] 3 times, *(3 dc, ch 2, 3 dc) in next corner ch-2 sp, ch 1, [3 dc in next ch-1 sp, ch 1] 3 times; rep from * twice more, 3 dc in beg sp, ch 2, join in 3rd ch of beg ch-3. Fasten off.

## SECOND MOTIF
Referring to Assembly Diagram for placement, work same as Rnds 1–8 of First Motif.
**Rnd 9 (joining rnd):** Ch 3, 2 dc in sp formed by joining sc, ch 1, **joining ch-2 sp** (see Special Stitches) 3 dc in same sp on working motif, [ch 1, sl st in next ch-1 sp on adjacent motif, 3 dc in next ch-1 sp on working motif] 3 times, ch 1, sl st in next ch-1 sp on adjacent motif, 3 dc in corner ch-2 sp, joining ch-2 sp, 3 dc in same sp on working motif, ch 1,

*[3 dc in next ch-1 sp, ch 1], 3 times, (3 dc, ch 2, 3 dc) in next corner, ch 1; rep from * once more, ch 1, [3 dc in next ch-1 sp, ch 1] 3 times, 3 dc in beg sp, ch 2, join in 3rd ch of beg ch-3. Fasten off.

## REMAINING MOTIFS

Referring to Assembly Chart for placement, work additional motifs as for Second Motif, joining to adjacent motifs in similar manner and making sure all 4-corner joinings are secure.

## BORDER

**Rnd 1:** Hold with RS and 1 short edge at top, join in corner ch-2 sp in upper right-hand corner, ch 3, 2 dc in same sp, ch 1, *[3 dc in next ch-1 sp, ch 1] 4 times, dc in next ch-2 sp, in motif joining and in ch-2 sp of next motif, ch 1; rep from * 3 times more, [3 dc in next ch-1 sp, ch 1] 4 times, (3 dc, ch 2, 3 dc) in corner ch-2 sp, ch 1, rep in similar manner around; 3 dc in beg sp, ch 1, join with sc in 3rd ch of beg ch-3 to form corner.

**Rnd 2:** Ch 3, 2 dc in sp formed by joining sc, ch 1, *(3 dc in next ch-1 sp, ch 1) in each ch-1 sp to next corner ch-2 sp, (3 dc, ch 2, 3 dc) in next ch-2 sp, rep from * around, ending 3 dc in beg sp, ch 1, join with sc in 3rd ch of beg ch-3.

**Rnd 3:** Rep Rnd 2.

**Rnd 4:** Ch 3, 3 dc in same sp, **picot** *(see Special Stitches),* sc in next ch-1 sp, *(3 dc, picot, 3 dc) in next ch-1 sp, sc in next ch-1 sp; rep from * around working (4 dc, picot, 4 dc) in each corner sp and ending (4 dc, picot) in beg sp, join in 3rd ch of beg ch-3.

Fasten off and weave in all ends. ❧

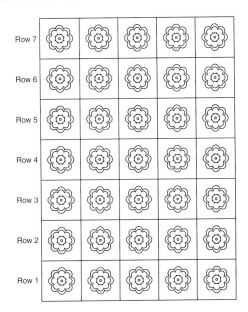

**Christening Rose**
Assembly Diagram

# GRACEFUL IVY

Design by Nanette Seale

## FINISHED SIZE
Approximately 45 x 58 inches

## MATERIALS
- Red Heart Super Saver medium (worsted) weight yarn (8 oz/452 yds/226g per skein): 6 skeins #661 frosty green
- Size H/8/5mm crochet hook or size needed to obtain gauge
- Tapestry needle

## GAUGE
Motif = 6½ inches square
To save time, take time to check gauge.

## PATTERN NOTE
Join with slip stitch unless otherwise stated.

## SPECIAL STITCHES
For **2-double crochet cluster (2-dc cl):** [Yo, insert hook in sp or st indicated, yo, pull up lp, yo, draw through 2 lps on hook] twice; yo and draw through all 3 lps on hook.

For **3-double crochet cluster (3-dc cl):** [Yo, insert hook in sp or st indicated, yo, pull up lp, yo, draw through 2 lps on hook] 3 times; yo and draw through all 4 lps on hook.

For **triple crochet cluster (tr cl):** *Yo twice, insert hook in sp or st indicated, yo, pull up lp, [yo, draw through 2 lps on hook] twice; rep from * as indicated to complete st, yo and draw through all lps on hook.

For **joining ch-3 sp:** Ch 1, sl st in corresponding ch-3 sp of adjacent motif, ch 1.

## FIRST MOTIF
**Rnd 1:** Make loose slip knot lp on hook, ch 2, dc in lp *(beg dc cl)*, [ch 2, **2-dc cl** *(see Special Stitches)* in lp] 7 times, ch 2; join top of beg dc cl. Tighten slip knot lp. *(8 cls)*

**Rnd 2:** Ch 6, **3-dc cl** *(see Special Stitches)* in 4th ch from hook, ch 1, *dc in next cl, ch 4, 3-dc cl in 4th ch from hook, ch 1; rep * around, join in 2nd ch of beg ch-6.

**Rnd 3:** Ch 6, sk first cl, *(**3-tr cl** *{see Special Stitches}*, ch 3, 3-tr cl, ch 3, 3-tr cl) in next dc *(corner)*, sk next cl, ch 3**, dc in next dc, ch 3, rep from * 3 times more, ending last rep at **, join in 3rd ch of beg ch-6.

**Rnd 4:** Ch 1, hdc in same st, 3 hdc in next ch-3 sp, hdc in next cl, 3 hdc in next ch-3 sp, *(hdc, ch-3, hdc) in corner cl, [3 hdc in next ch-3 sp, hdc in next cl] 3 times, 3 hdc in next ch-3 sp, rep from * twice more, (hdc, ch-3, hdc) in corner cl, 3 hdc in next ch-3 sp, hdc in next cl, 3 hdc in next ch-3 sp, join in first hdc.

**Rnd 5:** Ch 1, (sc, ch 3, sc) in same st, ch 3, 2-dc cl in 3rd ch from hook, sk next 3 hdc, *(sc, ch 3, sc) in next hdc, ch 3, 2-dc cl in 3rd ch from hook, sk next 4 hdc, (sc, ch 3, sc) in corner ch-3 sp, ch 3, 2-dc cl in 3rd ch from hook, sk next 4 hdc**, [(sc, ch 3, sc) in next hdc, ch 3, 2-dc cl in 3rd ch from hook, sk next 3 hdc] twice, rep from * 3 times more ending last rep at **, (sc, ch 3, sc) in next hdc, ch 3, 2-dc cl in 3rd ch from hook, sk next 3 hdc, join in first sc. Fasten off.

## SECOND MOTIF
Referring to Assembly Diagram for placement, work same as Rnds 1–4 of First Motif.

**Rnd 5 (joining rnd):** Ch 1, (sc, ch 3, sc) in same st, ch 3, 2-dc cl in 3rd ch from hook, sk next 3 hdc, (sc, ch 3, sc) in next hdc, ch 3, 2-dc cl in 3rd ch from hook, sk next 4 hdc, (sc, **joining ch-3 sp** *{see*

*Special Stitches},* sc) in corner ch-3 sp, ch 3, 2-dc cl in 3rd ch from hook, sk next 4 hdc, *(sc, joining ch-3 sp, sc) in next hdc, ch 3, 2-dc cl in 3rd ch from hook, sk next 3 hdc; rep from * once more, (sc, joining ch-3 sp, sc) in next hdc, ch 3, 2-dc cl in 3rd ch from hook, sk next 4 hdc, (sc, joining ch-3 sp, sc) in corner ch-3 sp, **ch 3, 2-dc cl in 3rd ch from hook, sk next 4 hdc, [(sc, ch 3, sc) in next hdc, ch 3, 2-dc cl in 3rd ch from hook, sk next 3 hdc] twice (sc, ch 3, sc) in next hdc, ch 3, 2-dc cl in 3rd ch from hook, sk next 4 hdc, (sc, ch 3, sc) in corner ch-3 sp, rep from ** once more, ch 3, 2-dc cl in 3rd ch from hook, sk next 4 hdc, (sc, ch 3, sc) in next hdc, ch 3, 2-dc cl in 3rd ch from hook, sk next 3 hdc, join in first sc. Fasten off.

## REMAINING MOTIFS

Referring to Assembly Diagram for placement, work rem motifs as for Second Motif, joining to adjacent motifs in similar manner and making sure all 4-corner joinings are secure.

## BORDER

**Rnd 1:** Hold with RS facing and one short end at top, join with sc in ch-3 sp in upper right-hand corner, *[ch 5, sc in next ch-3 sp] 4 times, ch 3, sc in ch-3 sp on next motif; rep from * to corner ch-3 sp, (sc, ch 3, sc) in corner ch-3 sp, rep in similar manner to beg corner, (sc, ch 3) in beg corner, join in first sc.

**Rnd 2:** Sl st in next ch-5 sp, ch 3, 2-dc cl, ch 2, [3-dc cl in same sp, ch 2] twice, *[(3-dc cl, ch 2) twice in next ch-5 lp] twice, (3-dc cl, ch 2) 3 times in next ch-5 lp, (3-dc cl, ch 2) in next ch-3 sp, (3-dc cl, ch 2) 3 times in next ch-5 lp; rep from * around, working (3-dc cl, ch 2, 3-dc cl) in each corner ch-3 sp, join in first 2-dc cl.

**Rnd 3:** Ch 1, sc in next ch-2 sp, *ch 3, 2-dc cl in 3rd ch from hook, sc in next ch-2 sp, rep from * around, join in first sc.
Fasten off and weave in all ends. 🐾

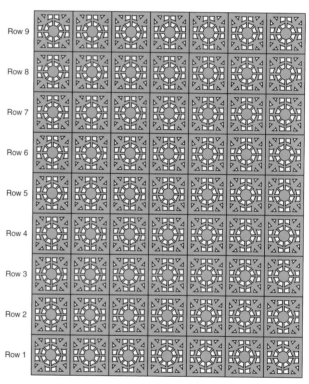

**Graceful Ivy**
Assembly Diagram

**SKILL LEVEL**
INTERMEDIATE

**YARN WEIGHT**
4 MEDIUM

# SUNSHINE SPLENDOR

Design by Joyce Nordstrom

## FINISHED SIZE

Approximately 52 x 60 inches

## MATERIALS

- Red Heart TLC Essentials, medium (worsted) weight yarn (6 oz/326 yds/170g per skein): 6 skeins butter #2220
- Size I/9/5.5mm crochet hook or size needed to obtain gauge

## GAUGE

Motif = 8½ inches
To save time, take time to check gauge.

## SPECIAL STITCH

For **shell:** (2 dc, ch 3, 2 dc) in sp or st indicated.

## PATTERN NOTES

Join with slip stitch unless otherwise stated.
Afghan is worked lengthwise in rows.

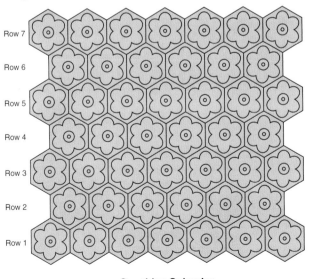

**Sunshine Splendor**
Assembly Diagram

## FIRST MOTIF

**Rnd 1:** Ch 4, join to form ring, ch 3 *(counts as dc throughout),* 17 dc in ring, join in 3rd ch of beg ch-3. *(18 dc)*

**Rnd 2:** Ch 3, dc in same st, working in **back lps** only, *sk next 2 dc, **shell** *(see Special Stitch)* in next st; rep from * 4 times more, sk next 2 dc, 2 dc in same st as beg ch 3, ch 1, join with hdc in 3rd ch of beg ch-3 to form beg shell. *(6 shells)*

**Rnd 3:** Ch 3, dc in sp formed by joining hdc, ch 3, 2 dc in same sp, *ch 3, sc between shells, ch 3, (2 dc, ch 3, 2 dc) in ch-3 sp of next shell; rep from * 4 times more, ch 3, sc between shells, ch 3, join in 3rd ch of beg ch-3.

**Rnd 4:** Sl st in next dc and in next ch-3 sp, ch 3, 10 dc in same sp; *ch 3, sc in next sc, ch 3, 11 dc in ch-3 sp of next shell; rep from * 4 times more, ch 3, sc in next sc, ch 3, join in 3rd ch of beg ch-3.

**Rnd 5:** Working in **back lps** only, *[sl st in next dc, ch 3, sk next dc] 6 times, sk next 2 ch-3 sps; rep from * 5 times more, join in first sl st.

**Rnd 6:** *Ch 3, sl st in next ch-3 sp; rep from * around, ending with ch-3, join in joining sl st. Fasten off.

## SECOND MOTIF

Referring to Assembly Diagram for placement, work same as Rnds 1–5 of First Motif.

**Rnd 6 (joining rnd):** [Ch 3, sl st in next ch-3 sp] 3 times, [ch 1, sl st in corresponding ch-3 sp of adjacent motif, ch 1, sl st in next ch-3 sp on working motif] 8 times, *ch 3, sl st in next ch-3 sp; rep from * around, ending with ch-3, join in joining sl st. Fasten off.

Continued on page 147

# PURPLE COMFORTS

Design by Linda Taylor

## FINISHED SIZE
Approximately 59 x 68 inches

## MATERIALS
- Plymouth Encore medium (worsted) weight yarn
  (3.5 oz/220 yds/100g per skein): 10 skeins #233
  pastel purple (A), 6 skeins each #208 white (B) and
  #1034 rich purple (C)
- Size I/9/5.5mm crochet hook or size needed to
  obtain gauge

## GAUGE
Motif = 4¼ inches
To save time, take time to check gauge.

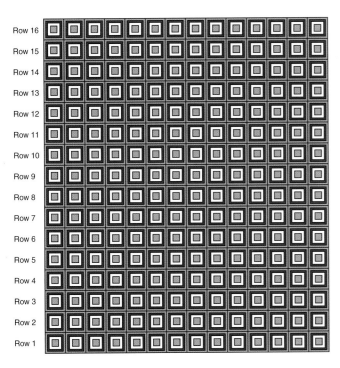

**Evening Reflections**
Assembly Diagram

Row 16
Row 15
Row 14
Row 13
Row 12
Row 11
Row 10
Row 9
Row 8
Row 7
Row 6
Row 5
Row 4
Row 3
Row 2
Row 1

## SPECIAL STITCHES
For **cluster (cl):** [Yo, insert hook in ring and draw up
lp] twice, yo and draw through all 5 lps on hook, ch 1.
For **joining ch-5 sp:** Ch 2, drop lp from hook, insert
hook in 3rd ch of corresponding ch-5 sp on adjacent
motif, pick up dropped lp and pull through, ch 2.
For **joining ch-2 sp:** Drop lp from hook, insert hook
in corresponding ch-2 sp on adjacent motif, pick up
dropped lp and pull through.

## PATTERN NOTE
Join with slip stitch unless otherwise stated.

## FIRST MOTIF
**Rnd 1:** With A, ch 4, join to form ring, *cl (see
Special Stitch) in ring, rep from * 7 times more; join in
top of first cl.

**Rnd 2:** Ch 1, sc in same cl, sc in sp between
cls, *sc in next cl, 3 sc in next sp (corner), sc in
next cl, sc in sp between cls; rep from * twice
more, sc in next cl, 3 sc in sp between cls, join in
first sc. Fasten off.

**Rnd 3:** Attach B in 3rd sc of any 3-sc corner, ch
2 (counts as dc), dc in next 4 sc, *(2 dc, ch 1, 2
dc) in next sc (corner), dc in next 5 sc; rep from
* twice more, (2 dc, ch 1, 2 dc) in corner, join in
2nd ch of beg ch 2. Fasten off.

**Rnd 4:** Attach C in 3rd dc from any corner ch-1
sp, ch 2 (counts as hdc), hdc next 6 dc, *(hdc,
ch 2, hdc) in corner ch-1 sp, sk next dc, hdc in
next 8 dc; rep from * twice more, (hdc, ch 2, hdc)
in corner ch-1 sp, sk next dc, hdc in next dc, join
in first hdc. Fasten off.

**Rnd 5:** Attach A in 2nd hdc from any ch-2 corner
sp, (sc, ch 2, hdc) in same st, *[sk next st, (sc,
ch 2, hdc) in next st] 3 times, (sc, ch 5, sc) in

corner ch-2 sp, [sk next st, (sc, ch 2, hdc) in next st] 4 times; rep from * twice more, (sc, ch 5, sc) in next corner ch-2 sp, join in first sc. Fasten off.

## SECOND MOTIF

Referring to Assembly Diagram for placement, work same as Rnds 1–4 of First Motif.

**Rnd 5 (joining rnd):** Attach A in 2nd hdc from any ch-2 corner sp, (sc, ch 2, hdc) in same st, [sk next st, (sc, ch 2, hdc) in next st] 3 times, (sc, **joining ch-5 sp** *{see Special Stitches}*, ch 2, sc) in next ch-2 corner sp, *sk next st, (sc, ch 2) in next st, **joining ch-2 sp** *(see Special Stitches)*, hdc in same st on working motif; rep from * 3 times more, sk next st, (sc, joining ch-5 sp, ch 2, sc) in next ch-2 corner sp, [sk next st, (sc, ch 2, hdc) in next st] 3 times, (sc, ch 5, sc) in corner ch-2 sp, [sk next st, (sc, ch 2, hdc) in next st] 4 times, (sc, ch 5, sc) in next corner ch-2 sp, join in first sc. Fasten off.

## REMAINING MOTIFS

Referring to Assembly Diagram for placement, work as for Second Motif, joining to adjacent motifs in similar manner and making sure all 4-corner joinings are secure.

Weave in all ends. ❧

# SUNSHINE SPLENDOR Continued from page 143

## REMAINING MOTIFS

Referring to Assembly Diagram for placement, work rem motifs as for Second Motif, joining to corresponding sides of adjacent motifs in similar manner.

## BORDER

**Note:** *For dec: Yo, pull up lp in corner ch-3 sp of working motif, yo, pull up lp in corner ch-3 sp of next motif, yo and draw through all 3 lps on hook.*

**Rnd 1:** Attach yarn with sc in any ch-3 sp, ch 3, *[sc in next ch-3 sp, ch 3] to motif joining, **dec** *(see Note)* over joining, ch 3; rep from * around, ending last rep with ch 3, join in first sc.

**Rnd 2:** Sl st in next ch-3 sp, ch 1, sc in same sp, *ch 3, sc in next ch-3 sp; rep from * around, join in first sc.

**Rnd 3:** Sl st in next ch-3 sp, ch 1, sl st in same sp, *ch 1, sk next sc, (sl st, ch 1, sl st) in next ch-3 sp; rep from * around, ch 1, join in first sl st.

Fasten off and weave in all ends. ❧

# TANTALIZING THYME

Design by Joyce Nordstrom

## FINISHED SIZE
Approximately 52 x 63 inches

## MATERIALS
- Red Heart TLC Essentials medium (worsted) weight yarn (6 oz/326 yds/170g per skein): 3 skeins each #2672 light thyme (B) and #2673 medium thyme (C), 2 skeins each #2675 dark thyme (D) and #2316 winter white (A)
- Size I/9/5.5mm crochet hook or sized needed to obtain gauge

## GAUGE
Motif = 5½ inches square
To save time, take time to check gauge.

## SPECIAL STITCHES
For **beginning cluster (beg cl):** Keeping last lp of each dc on hook, 2 dc in st or sp indicated, yo and draw through all 3 lps on hook.

For **cluster (cl):** Ch 3, keeping last lp of each dc on hook, 3 dc in st or sp indicated, yo and draw through all 4 lps on hook.

## PATTERN NOTES
Join with slip stitch unless otherwise noted.
Refer to layout diagram for Motif color.

## FIRST MOTIF
**Rnd 1 (RS):** With A, ch 4, join to form a ring, **beg cl** (see Special Stitches) in ring, [ch 3, **cl** (see Special Stitches) in ring] 7 times, ch 1, join with hdc in top of beg cl. (8 cls)

**Rnd 2:** Beg cl over joining hdc, *ch 3, sc in next ch-3 sp, ch 3, [cl, ch 3, cl] in next ch-3 sp (corner); rep from * twice more, ch 3, sc in next ch-3 sp, ch 3, cl in next sp, ch 1, join with hdc in top of beg cl.

**Rnd 3:** Beg cl over joining hdc, *[ch 3, sc in next ch-3 sp] twice, ch 3, (cl, ch 3, cl) in corner ch-3 sp; rep from * twice more, [ch 3, sc in next ch-3 sp] twice, ch 3, cl in next sp, ch 1, join with hdc in top of beg cl.

**Rnd 4:** Beg cl over joining hdc, *[ch 3, sc in next ch-3 sp] 3 times, ch 3, [cl, ch 3, cl] in corner ch-3 sp; rep from * twice more, [ch 3, sc in next ch-3 sp] 3 times, ch 3, cl in next ch-3 sp, ch 1, join with hdc in top of beg cl. Fasten off.

## SECOND MOTIF
Referring to Assembly Diagram for color and placement, work same as Rnds 1–3 of First Motif.

**Rnd 4 (joining rnd):** Beg cl over joining hdc, [ch 3, sc in next ch-3 sp] 3 times, ch 3, [cl, ch 3, cl] in corner ch-3 sp, [ch 3, sc in next ch-3 sp] 3 times, ch 3, cl in corner ch-3 sp, ch 1, sl st in corresponding corner ch-3 sp on adjacent motif; ch 1, cl in same sp on working motif, [ch 1, sl st in corresponding ch-3 sp of adjacent motif, ch 1, sl st in next ch-3 sp on working motif] 3 times, ch 1, sl st in corresponding ch-3 sp on adjacent motif, ch 1, cl in next ch-3 sp on working motif, ch 1, sl st in corresponding corner ch-3 sp on adjacent motif, ch 1, cl in corner ch-3 sp on working motif, [ch 3, sc in next ch-3 sp] 3 times, ch 3, cl in next ch-3 sp, ch 1, join with hdc in top of beg cl. Fasten off.

## REMAINING MOTIFS

Referring to Assembly Diagram for color and placement, work same as Second Motif, joining to adjacent motifs in similar manner and making sure all 4-corner joinings are secure.

## BORDER

**Rnd 1:** With RS facing, attach A in any corner ch-3 sp, beg cl in same sp, *[ch 3, sc in next ch-3 sp] 4 times, ch 3, sc in motif joining; rep from * across to last motif, [ch 3, sc in next ch-3 sp] 4 times, ch 3, (cl, ch 3, cl) in corner ch-3 sp; rep from * in similar manner around joining in top of beg cl. Fasten off.

**Rnd 2:** Attach B in any corner ch-3 sp, beg cl in same sp, *[ch 3, sc in next ch-3 sp] to next corner, ch 3, (cl, ch 3, cl) in corner ch-3 sp; rep from * twice more, [ch 3, sc in next ch-3 sp] to next corner, ch 3, (cl, ch 3) in same sp as beg cl, sl st in top of beg cl. Fasten off.

**Rnd 3:** With C, rep Rnd 2.

**Rnd 4:** Attach D in any corner ch-3 sp, beg cl in same sp, *[ch-3, sc in next ch 3 sp, ch 3, cl in next ch-3 sp] to corner ch-3 sp, ch 3, (cl, ch 3, cl) in corner sp; rep from * twice more, [ch 3, sc in next ch-3 sp, ch 3, cl in next ch-3 sp] to beg corner, ch 3, (cl, ch 3) in beg corner, join in top of beg cl.

Fasten off and weave in all ends. 🦐

**COLOR KEY**
- ☐ Winter White
- ▨ Light Thyme
- ▨ Medium Thyme
- ■ Dark Thyme

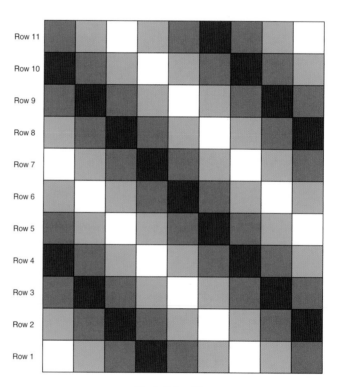

**Tantalizing Thyme**
Assembly Diagram

# BLUE STREAKS

Design by Bonnie Pierce

## FINISHED SIZE
Approximately 34 x 48 inches

## MATERIALS
- Red Heart Super Saver medium (worsted) weight yarn (3 oz/170 yds/85g per skein): 8 skeins #827 light periwinkle
- Size G/6/4mm crochet hook
- Size H/8/5mm crochet hook or size needed to obtain gauge

## GAUGE
Motif = 7 inches square
To save time, take time to check gauge.

## SPECIAL STITCHES
For **roll stitch (roll st):** Yo 6 times loosely and evenly; insert hook into st indicated, yo, draw up lp, yo, draw through 7 lps (wiggling the hook and rolling the yarn back and forth), yo and draw through 2 lps on hook.

For **2-double crochet cluster (2-dc cl):** Keeping last lp of each dc on hook, 2 dc in st or sp indicated, yo and draw through all 3 lps on hook.

For **4-double crochet cluster (4-dc cl):** Keeping last lp of each dc on hook [2 dc in next 2-dc cl] twice, yo and draw through all 5 lps on hook.

## PATTERN NOTE
Join with slip stitch unless otherwise stated.

## FIRST MOTIF
**Rnd 1:** With smaller hook, make slip knot on hook, ch 2, [**roll st** *(see Special Stitches)* in slip knot lp] 12 times. Tighten slip knot lp.

**Rnd 2:** With larger hook, ch 3 *(counts as dc)*, dc in same sp, ch 2, **2-dc cl** *(see Special Stitches)* in next st, ch 2, *dc in next st, ch 2, [2-dc cl in next st, ch 2] twice; rep from * twice more, dc in next st, ch 2, join in 3rd ch of beg ch-3.

**Rnd 3:** Ch 3, keeping last lp of each dc on hook, dc in same st, 2 dc in next cl, yo and draw through all 4 lps on hook *(beg 4-dc cl)*, *ch 3, (dc, ch 4, dc) in next dc *(corner)*, ch 3, **4-dc cl** *(see Special Stitches)* over next two 2-dc cls; rep from * twice more, (dc, ch 4, dc) in next dc *(corner)*, ch 3, join in top of beg 4-dc cl.

**Rnd 4:** Sl st in next ch-3 sp, ch 1, 4 sc in same sp, dc in next dc, (3 dc, ch 3, 3 dc) in next corner ch-4 sp, dc in next dc, *[4 sc in next ch-3 sp] twice, dc in next dc, (3 dc, ch 3, 3 dc) in next corner ch-4 sp, dc in next dc; rep from * twice more, 4 sc in next ch-3 sp, join in first sc.

**Rnd 5:** Ch 1, sc in same sc and in next 7 sts, *3 sc in next corner ch-3 sp, sc in next 16 sts; rep from * twice more, sc in next 8 sts, join in first sc.

**Rnd 6:** Sl st in next sc, ch 3 *(counts as hdc and ch-1 sp)*, [sk next st, hdc in next st, ch 1] 3 times, (hdc, ch 2, hdc) in corner sc, *ch 1, hdc in next sc, [ch 1, sk next sc, hdc in next sc] 8 times, ch 1, (hdc, ch 2, hdc) in next corner sc; rep from * twice more, hdc in next sc, [ch 1, sk next st, hdc in next sc] 4 times, ch 1, join in 2nd ch of beg ch-3.

**Rnd 7:** Sl st in next ch-1 sp, ch 1, 2 sc in same sp and in each ch-1 sp around, working 3 sc in each corner. Fasten off.

## SECOND MOTIF
Referring to Assembly Diagram for placement, work same as Rnds 1–6 of First Motif. At end of Rnd 6, fasten off.

**Rnd 7 (joining rnd):** Join in corner ch-2 sp, sc in

same sp, *2 sc in each ch-1 sp to next corner, 3 sc in corner ch-2 sp; rep from * once more, 2 sc in each ch-1 sp, sc in corner ch-2 sp, holding working motif and adjacent motif with RS tog and working on WS through both motifs, 2 sc in same corner, in each ch-1 sp across, and in next corner. Fasten off.

## REMAINING MOTIFS

Referring to Assembly Diagram for placement, work additional motifs as for Second Motif, joining to form first row. For rem rows join in similar manner to adjacent motif and previous row, making sure all 4-corner joinings are secure.

## BORDER

**Rnd 1:** Hold with RS facing and 1 short edge at top, join with sc in center sc in upper right-hand corner, 2 sc in same sp, sc in each st around working 3 sc in each corner; join in first sc.

**Rnd 2:** Ch 1, sc in each sc, working 3 sc in each corner; join in first sc.

Fasten off and weave in all ends. ❧

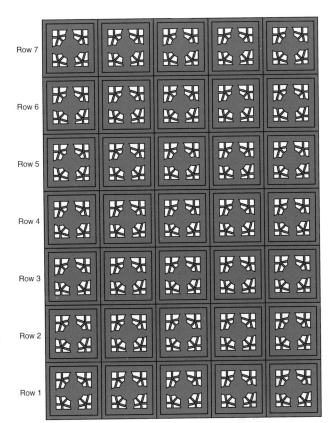

**Blue Streaks**
Assembly Diagram

# EVENING REFLECTIONS

Design by Joyce Nordstrom

## FINISHED SIZE
Approximately 53 x 64 inches

## MATERIALS
- TLC Amore medium (worsted) weight yarn (6 oz/ 290 yds/170g per skein): 8 skeins #3220 wheat
- Size I/9/5.5mm crochet hook or size needed to obtain gauge

## GAUGE
Motif = 10 inches square
To save time, take time to check gauge.

## SPECIAL STITCHES
For **shell:** (2 dc, ch 1, 2 dc) in same sp or st.
For **V-stitch (V-st):** (Dc, ch 1, dc) in same sp or st.
For **cluster (cl):** Yo, pull up lp in same sp, yo, pull up lp in next sp, yo and draw through all 5 lps on hook, ch 1.

## PATTERN NOTE
Join with slip stitch unless otherwise stated.

## FIRST MOTIF

**Rnd 1 (RS):** Ch 6, join to form a ring, ch 4 *(counts as a tr and ch-2 sp),* [tr in ring, ch 2] 10 times, tr, ch 1, join with hdc in 3rd ch of beg ch-4. *(12 tr)*

**Rnd 2:** Ch 3 *(counts as dc),* dc in sp formed by joining hdc; *[ch 1, sk next tr, 2 dc in next ch-2 sp] twice, ch 1**, [2 dc, ch 2, 2 dc] in next sp *(corner);* rep from * 3 times more ending last rep at **; 2 dc in next sp, ch 1, join with hdc in 3rd ch of beg ch-3.

**Rnd 3:** Ch 3, (dc, ch 1, 2 dc) in sp formed by joining hdc *(beg shell),* *sk next two 2-dc groups, **shell** *(see Special Stitches)* in sp between 2-dc groups**, (shell, ch 2, shell) in corner ch-2 sp; rep from * 3 times more, ending last rep at **; shell in corner ch-2 sp, ch 1, join with hdc in 3rd ch of beg ch-3.

**Rnd 4:** Ch 3, dc in sp formed by joining hdc, *[ch 1, shell in ch-1 sp of next shell] 3 times, ch 1**, [2 dc, ch 2, 2 dc] in corner ch-2 sp, rep from * 3 times more, ending last rep at **, 2 dc in corner ch-2 sp, ch 1, join with hdc in 3rd ch of beg ch-3.

**Rnd 5:** Ch 3, (dc, ch 1, 2 dc) in sp formed by joining hdc, *[ch 1, shell in ch-1 sp of next shell] 3 times**, (shell, ch 2, shell) in corner ch-2 sp, rep from * 3 times more, ending last rep at **, shell in corner ch-2 sp, ch 1, join with hdc in 3rd ch of beg ch-3. **Turn.**

**Rnd 6 (WS):** Ch 4 *(counts as dc and ch-1 sp),* dc in sp formed by joining hdc *(beg V-st),* *ch 1, [**V-st** *(see Special Stitches)* in ch-1 sp of shell, ch 1, dc between shells, ch 1] 4 times, V-st in ch-1 sp of next shell**; [V-st, ch 2, V-st] in corner sp, rep from * 3 times more, ending last rep at **, V-st in corner ch-2 sp, ch 1, join with hdc in 3rd ch of beg ch-4. **Turn.**

**Rnd 7 (RS):** Ch 1, *[**cl** *(see Special Stitches)*] 18 times; ch 2 *(corner);* rep from * 3 times more; join in top of first cl. Fasten off.

## SECOND MOTIF

***Note:*** *While working joining rnd, corresponding shells should create a continuous line.*
Referring to Assembly Diagram for placement, work same as Rnds 1–6 of First Motif.

**Rnd 7 (joining rnd):** Ch 1, [**cl** *(see Special Stitches)*] 18 times; ch 1, sl st in corresponding corner ch-2 sp on adjacent motif, [cl on working motif, ch 1, sl st in corresponding sp of adjacent motif] across, ch 1, sl st in corner ch-2 sp on adjacent motif, *[cl] 18 times, ch 2 *(corner)*; rep from * once more, join in top of first cl. Fasten off.

### REMAINING MOTIFS

Referring to Assembly Diagram for placement, work as for Second Motif, joining to adjacent motifs in similar manner and making sure all 4-corner joinings are secure.

### BORDER

**Rnd 1 (WS):** Hold with WS facing, attach in any corner ch-2 sp, ch 1, cl over corner and ch-1 of next cl, *[cl in each cl and in each joining] to corner; [cl, ch 2, cl, ch 2, cl] in corner, rep from *around, ending last cl, ch 1, join with hdc in first cl. **Turn.**

**Rnd 2 (RS):** Ch 1, cl over corner and ch-1 of next cl, *[cl] to corner; [cl, ch 1, cl, ch 2, cl, ch 1, cl] in corner, rep from *around, ending last cl with ch 1, join in first cl. **Do not turn.**

**Rnd 3:** Working from left to right, [sc in next ch-1 sp, ch 1] around.

Fasten off and weave in ends. ❧

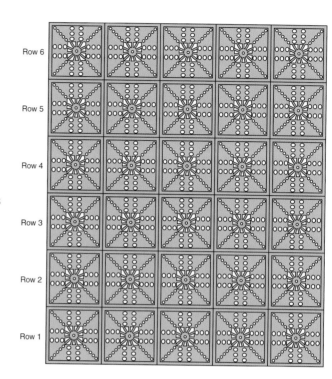

**Evening Reflections**
Assembly Diagram

# ABBREVIATIONS & SYMBOLS

| | |
|---|---|
| beg | beg/beginning |
| bpdc | back post double crochet |
| bphdc | back post half double crochet |
| bpsc | back post single crochet |
| bptr | back post treble crochet |
| CC | contrasting color |
| ch | chain stitch |
| ch- | refers to chain or space previously made (i.e. ch-1 space) |
| ch sp | chain space |
| cl(s) | cluster(s) |
| cm | centimeters(s) |
| dc | double crochet |
| dec | decrease/decreases/decreasing |
| dtr | double treble crochet |
| fpdc | front post double crochet |
| fphdc | front post half double crochet |
| fpsc | front post single crochet |
| fptr | front post treble crochet |
| g | gram(s) |
| hdc | half double crochet |
| inc | increase/increases/increasing |
| lp(s) | loop(s) |
| MC | main color |
| mm | millimeter(s) |
| oz | ounce(s) |
| pc | popcorn |
| rem | rem/remaining |
| rep | repeat(s) |
| rnd(s) | round(s) |
| RS | right side |
| sc | single crochet |
| sk | skip |
| sl st | slip stitch |
| sp(s) | space(s) |
| st(s) | stitch(es) |
| tog | together |
| tr | treble crochet |
| trtr | triple treble crochet |
| WS | wrong side |
| yd(s) | yard(s) |
| yo | yarn over |

**\* An asterisk** is used to mark the beginning of a portion of instructions to be worked more than once; thus, "rep from \* twice more" means after working the instructions once, repeat the instructions following the asterisk twice more (3 times in all).

**[ ] Brackets** are used to enclose instructions that are to be worked the number of times indicated after the brackets. For example, "[2 dc in next st, sk next st] 5 times" means to follow the instructions within the brackets a total of 5 times.

**( ) Parentheses** are used to enclose a group of stitches that are worked in one space or stitch. For example, "(2 dc, ch 2, 2 dc) in next st" means to work all the stitches within the parentheses in the next space or stitch. Parentheses are also used to enclose special instructions or stitch counts.

## Skill Levels

| ◧□□▷ | ◧◧□▷ | ◧◧◧▷ | ◧◧◧◨ |
|---|---|---|---|
| **BEGINNER** | **EASY** | **INTERMEDIATE** | **EXPERIENCED** |
| Beginner projects for first-time crocheters using basic stitches. Minimal shaping. | Easy projects using basic stitches, repetitive stitch patterns, simple color changes and simple shaping and finishing. | Intermediate projects with a variety of stitches, mid-level shaping and finishing. | Experienced projects using advanced techniques and stitches, detailed shaping and refined finishing. |

# Standard Yarn Weight System

Categories of yarn, gauge ranges, and recommended needle and hook sizes

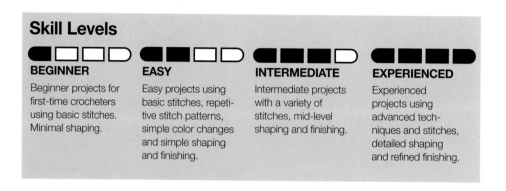

| Yarn Weight Symbol & Category Names | 1 SUPER FINE | 2 FINE | 3 LIGHT | 4 MEDIUM | 5 BULKY | 6 SUPER BULKY |
|---|---|---|---|---|---|---|
| Type of Yarns in Category | Sock, Fingering, Baby | Sport, Baby | DK, Light Worsted | Worsted, Afghan, Aran | Chunky, Craft, Rug | Super Chunky, Roving |
| Crochet Gauge* Ranges in Single Crochet to 4 inch | 21–32 sts | 16–20 sts | 12–17 sts | 11–14 sts | 8–11 sts | 5–9 sts |
| Recommended Hook in Metric Size Range | 2.25–3.5 mm | 3.5–4.5 mm | 4.5–5.5 mm | 5.5–6.5 mm | 6.5–9 mm | 9 mm and larger |
| Recommended Hook U.S. Size Range | B-1–E-4 | E-4–7 | 7–I-9 | I-9–K-10½ | K-10½–M-13 | M-13 and larger |

\* GUIDELINES ONLY: The above reflect the most commonly used gauges and hook sizes for specific yarn categories.

# CROCHET STITCH GUIDE

## CROCHET HOOKS

| Metric | US | Metric | US |
|--------|-----|--------|------|
| .60mm | 14 | 3.00mm | D/3 |
| .75mm | 12 | 3.50mm | E/4 |
| 1.00mm | 10 | 4.00mm | F/5 |
| 1.50mm | 6 | 4.50mm | G/6 |
| 1.75mm | 5 | 5.00mm | H/8 |
| 2.00mm | B/1 | 5.50mm | I/9 |
| 2.50mm | C/2 | 6.00mm | J/10 |

**Chain—ch:** Yo, pull through lp on hook.

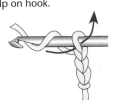

**Slip stitch—sl st:** Insert hook in st, yo, pull through both lps on hook.

**Front loop—front lp Back loop—back lp**

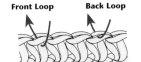

**Single crochet—sc:** Insert hook in st, yo, pull through st, yo, pull through both lps on hook.

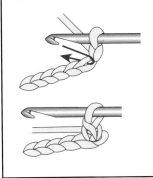

**Reverse single crochet— reverse sc:** Working from left to right, insert hook in next st, complete as sc.

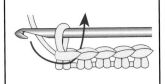

**Front post stitch—fp: Back post stitch—bp:** When working post st, insert hook from right to left around post st on previous row.

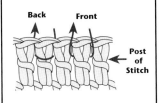

**Half double crochet—hdc:** Yo, insert hook in st, yo, pull through st, yo, pull through all 3 lps on hook.

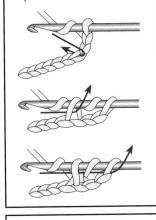

**Double crochet—dc:** Yo, insert hook in st, yo, pull through st, [yo, pull through 2 lps] twice.

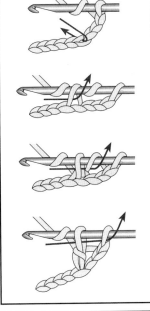

**Change colors:** Drop first color; with second color, pull through last 2 lps of st.

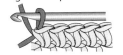

**Treble crochet—tr:** Yo twice, insert hook in st, yo, pull through st, [yo, pull through 2 lps] 3 times.

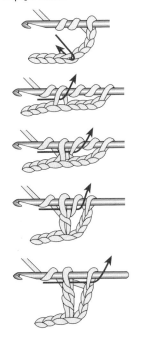

**Double treble crochet— dtr:** Yo 3 times, insert hook in st, yo, pull through st, [yo, pull through 2 lps] 4 times.

**Single crochet decrease (sc dec):** (Insert hook, yo, draw up a lp) in each of the sts indicated, yo, draw through all lps on hook.

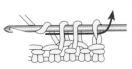

Example of 2-sc dec

**Half double crochet decrease (hdc dec):** (Yo, insert hook, yo, draw lp through) in each of the sts indicated, yo, draw through all lps on hook.

**Double crochet decrease (dc dec):** (Yo, insert hook, yo, draw lp through, yo, draw through 2 lps on hook) in each of the sts indicated, yo, draw through all lps on hook.

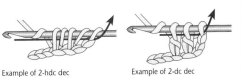

Example of 2-hdc dec          Example of 2-dc dec

| US | UK |
|----|-----|
| sl st (slip stitch) | = sc (single crochet) |
| sc (single crochet) | = dc (double crochet) |
| hdc (half double crochet) | = htr (half treble crochet) |
| dc (double crochet) | = tr (treble crochet) |
| tr (treble crochet) | = dtr (double treble crochet) |
| dtr (double treble crochet) | = ttr (triple treble crochet) |
| skip | = miss |

For more complete information, visit

**StitchGuide.com**

# Special Thanks

We would like to thank the talented crochet designers whose work is featured in this collection.

**Carol Alexander**
Roses Are Blue, 9
Passion for Purple, 16
Pure Pleasure, 30

**Donna Collinsworth**
Be My Valentine, 121

**Katharine Eng**
Spring Floral, 19

**Kathleen Garen**
Spring Bouquet, 124

**Tammy Hildebrand**
Wedding Wreaths, 35
Bursts of Fur, 66
Luscious Limes, 69
Velvety Roses, 72
Bebop Blocks, 75
Diagonal Dots, 81
Sunshine & Lace, 111
Pink Petals, 117

**Maria Merlino**
Patriot's Picnic, 127
Poinsettia Beauties, 133
Christening Rose, 137

**Joyce Nordstrom**
Lily Hexagons, 12
Sophisticated Zigzag, 43
Spring Plaid, 53
Diamond Bouclé, 96
Ball Game, 108
Sunshine Splendor, 143
Tantalizing Thyme, 148
Evening Reflections, 154

**Bonnie Pierce**
Sweet Imagination, 27
Violet Vision, 32
Zigzag Squares, 90
Roll Stitch Rhapsody, 93
Berries & Cream, 99
Blue Streaks, 151

**Diane Poellot**
Sunny Day Flowers, 6
Dream Garden, 39

**Nanette Seale**
Make Me Smile, 114
Graceful Ivy, 140

**Darla Sims**
Overlapping Squares, 59
Mystical Mist, 78
Medley in Blue, 85
Gracious Garden, 88
Playful Colors, 106

**Ann E. Smith**
Blazing Embers, 46
Log Cabin Inspiration, 56
Stair Steps, 103

**Martha Brooks Stein**
Brilliant Butterfly, 50

**Brenda Stratton**
Desert Flowers, 22

**Kathleen Stuart**
Fall Foliage, 130

**Linda Taylor**
Purple Comforts, 145